CASTING DIRECTORS' SECRETS

CASTING DIRECTORS' SECRETS

Inside Tips for Successful Auditions

GINGER HOWARD FRIEDMAN

LIMELIGHT EDITIONS

First Limelight Edition December 2004
© 2004 Ginger Howard Friedman
© 2000 Ginger Howard

Published by:
    LIMELIGHT EDITIONS (an imprint of Amadeus Press)
    512 Newark Pompton Turnpike
    Pompton Plains, New Jersey 07444, USA
    www.limelighteditions.com

For sales, please contact:
    LIMELIGHT EDITIONS
    c/o Hal Leonard Corporation
    7777 West Bluemound Road
    Milwaukee, Wisconsin 53213, USA
    TEL. 800-637-2852
    FAX 414-774-3259

Printed in the United States of America

The Library of Congress has cataloged the original edition as follows:

Howard, Ginger–
Casting directors' secrets : inside tips for successful auditions / Ginger Howard.
p. cm.
Includes index.
ISBN 1-58115-072-5
1. Acting—Auditions. i. Title
PN2071.A92 H69 2000
792'.028 DC21 00-059393

Taking A Bow

Singer Howard Freedman

For acting students everywhere: Courage.
and for Chloe Mae Bennett Friedman

"To thine own self be true."
W. S.

"This does not mean to be self-indulgent."
G. H. F.

Contents

ACKNOWLEDGEMENTS

I WOULD LIKE TO EXPRESS MY PROFOUND APPRECIATION TO Michael Shurtleff; casting director of all casting directors; the original; innovator, visionary, and architect of professionally and methodically run casting sessions. Actors, casting directors, producers, directors, writers, and audiences continue to benefit from his wisdom. If not for him, I wouldn't have become a casting director, acting teacher, and author of three acting books; he changed the course of my life and enhanced it immeasurably. I am forever in his debt for giving me the opportunity to work for him, to learn from him, and to enjoy the privilege of his friendship.

And also for being the best damn dancing partner of them all.

For every production, there is a director. This person should be thought of by his or her flock (the actors) as Solomon, Moses, Jesus, Freud, and Henry Kissinger all rolled into one.

The success of the performances and the entire production depends on the guidance and inspiration imparted by the director.

So it is for the writer. Every author has a director to guide, provoke, and inspire. In publishing she or he is called an editor. I am and shall be forever indebted to my director/editor, Nicole Potter, who received pages and turned them into a book. She put me to task on revisions, but my work did not exceed the time and effort invested by her. I thank her for teaching me how to be better at what I do.

I'd like to thank the following American and Canadian casting directors for their invaluable contribution to this book. I have complied with those requesting that their names be omitted.

Craig Alexander Casting
Michelle Allen Casting, Inc.
Deborah Barylski Casting: *Just Shoot Me, Home Improvement*
Jo Edna Boldin Casting
John Buchan, Alliance Productions
Donald Case Casting, Inc.
Marsha Chesley Casting
Leonard Finger Casting
Stephanie Gorin & Associates: *Forever Swing, Lion King, Rent, Cirque du Soleil, Beauty and the Beast, I Love You, You're Perfect, Now Change, Forever Plaid;* television: *Naked City;* plus dozens more theatre, film, and television productions
Deborah Green, Rocky Mountain Casting
Judy Henderson Casting
Stuart Howard Associates
Lisa Miller Katz, Katz Casting: *Everybody Loves Raymond, The King of Queens*
Juli-Ann Kay, Ross Clydesdale Casting, and Shannon C. Klasell, Donald Case Casting, Inc.
Sid Kozak, KPS Casting
Cheryl Louden-Kubin, The Casting Crew, Inc.

Shasta Lutz, Jigsaw Casting

Louise Mackiewicz, The Casting Line Canada, Inc.:
     commercials

Kelly McLaughlin, Comerford Casting, Inc.

Sandi Nielsen, Best Side Casting

Christy L. Pokarney, Omega Entertainment

Liz Ramos Casting

Patricia Rose Casting

Jann Stefoff, Allsorts Casting

Clare Walker Casting, Inc.

Cathy Weseluck, Chatterbox Productions

My thanks to Shelley Zane for assisting me with those follow-up phone calls to casting directors.

INTRODUCTION

"**Y**OU GOT THE PART."

I've always said that these are the most beautiful words an actor can hear. If you have been the recipient of these four words, you know the feeling of personal (and professional) triumph.

You got the part for one reason. You were the best candidate for the part. You were not only the best; your reading was brilliant! The competition was fierce; it appeared to you that everyone of your type and age range in the city was auditioning for the same part, but *you* got it!

The part became yours because life-and-death choices were made by you for the character, and a strong inner life was created. You had total commitment to your character and to the relationship between the two characters on the pages. You aggressively *listened* to the other character's words before responding; you *reacted*. You made *the here and now* the most important moment in your character's life. You created powerful *emotional reach-out, emotional power, emotional action*, and *emotional honesty*. The casting director believed every word you said; therefore, you got the part! That's the bottom line, you know. If they believe you, chances are you will get a callback and the part.

You also arrived well in advance of your scheduled appointment (clothed in what you *felt* the character might be wearing), checked in with the monitor, and spent your valuable time in the waiting area preparing with the audition sides. You entered the audition room in a pleasant manner, somewhat in character, stood where you were told to, did your slate properly (for a camera audition), and proceeded with the reading, making sure, throughout, that you made ample eye contact with and a connection to the reader.

At the conclusion of your reading, you gathered your belongings from the nearby chair, said good-bye with a smile, and left.

The irony is that you were not exactly the age or type they were looking for, but you gave the *best* reading! Astute casting directors and directors understand that *talent becomes type.*

Many years ago I auditioned for a featured part in a Broadway play. I didn't get the part. I went to see the play and exclaimed afterward that *I* was much better than the actress who did get the part. It took several years of maturing on my part to realize that if I were better, it would have been me up there on that stage playing eight performances a week in scenes with Sir Alec Guinness, not her. There was no doubt that she got the part because of her superior reading. But at the time my unrealistic sentiments compensated for my utter feelings of rejection.

Don't delude yourself as I did. You will get the part if your performance was the best. It's as simple as that.

However, be advised that when it comes down to two actors for a featured or lead part, the actor with the stronger résumé will usually be cast. The reason is that the more experienced actor has already proven himself or herself to be reliable. If the project is a major production, the producer feels more secure with a tried-and-true actor.

This book is directed toward the actor who is about to embark on auditions and for the actor who has gone through a series of auditions with little success.

These pages should be read by acting students currently in acting programs in colleges, acting schools, and high schools. What I present should be utilized as part of the acting student's learning process. For actors who have completed their acting training, this book is vital because the acting teacher is not involved in the casting process and is therefore ill-equipped to advise the actor on audition technique and what is expected of the actor at various types of auditions. The casting director who is endowed with *teaching* skills (two different disciplines) is the correct one to teach, counsel, and advise actors on acting for auditions. Even very good actors with degrees from fine acting programs make mistakes at their auditions.

On these pages casting directors from America and Canada explain for the first time why actors get hired, why actors get rejected, what the casting directors want, and what they don't want. They reveal the mistakes made by actors, including the three most common blunders at auditions for theatre, film, and television. Finally, actors will learn what casting directors have to say about all the ways in which actors sabotage their own auditions. The secrets are out! The casting directors tell all!

Acts of sabotage can be committed before, during, and at the conclusion of the audition. I have full knowledge of every aspect of the casting system in the United States and Canada. I am personally aware of the mistakes made by actors. I've made some of them myself! It appears that actors can be very creative about screwing up at the audition. All of the common mistakes committed by auditioners are on these pages. Other casting directors and I present over a hundred ways to correct these mistakes. We teach you how to make sure you *never* make these mistakes at your auditions.

I am grateful to the casting directors who magnanimously offered to share their findings with me so that I may pass them on to you. The knowledgeable and professionally behaved actor will, after all, make the casting directors' lives easier while reaping great rewards for himself or herself.

Every possible mistake that can be humanly committed at your audition is listed on these pages; all from the mouths of working, respected, high-powered casting directors.

Casting directors are the people who grant you the audition after you have been submitted by your agent. The casting director represents the production you are auditioning for. As Patricia Rose states, the casting director is "the gatekeeper."

One becomes a casting director by starting as a switchboard operator in a producer's office, a secretary in a production company or for a casting director, an assistant, a gofer, an unpaid apprentice, or an agent who prefers representing a production over a group of actors.

I had the inclinations of a casting director without realizing it before I even knew there was such a position. I would privately cast every book I read. From childhood until my working days, I saw *every* movie produced! These days I am much more selective.

While reading an advanced copy of *The Godfather,* I knew before I reached the halfway mark that the only actor to play the lead was Marlon Brando. I conveyed my thoughts to the writer of the book, Mario Puzo, who was a friend, and of course, even though I was not the casting director for the film, Mr. Brando did indeed get the part.

The casting director must have at his or her disposal a comprehensive file of each and every acting candidate locally (in major film and theatre offices, the file is international) of every type, age range, race, and gender; of every musical, dramatic, and comedic ability. These extensive files also contain the actors' experiences, agents, and personal comments made by the casting director.

The casting director auditions several actors in the file before honoring the agent's submission, in order to screen out the actors and to keep the files updated, full, and active. Other actors will be auditioning for the casting director for the first time at the casting session.

The casting director will grant an audition to an actor not previously screened when there is respect and trust toward the agent submitting the actor. A responsible agent will only submit an actor who is the type being sought and whose résumé reflects adequate and appropriate credits; the thinking agent is not about to waste the casting director's time and risk his or her own reputation and career with frivolous submissions.

However, a creative and courageous agent, with knowledge of a director's inventive and risk-taking casting, will submit a client who, while totally at variance with the character breakdown, is nevertheless endowed with powerful acting skills; the *talent* becomes the type!

Manny Azenberg, a prolific and brilliant Broadway producer, replaced Tom Conti with Mary Tyler Moore in *Whose Life Is It Anyway?* There was much laughter from members of the theatre community (including this writer) upon hearing about this "ill-fitting" choice. After all, she is a comedic actress, and this is heavy drama; *and* the part was written for a man! However, after viewing Ms. Moore in the play, all laughter was replaced with reverence for her and for Mr. Azenberg by theatergoers and critics. Suddenly we changed our tune to "What a stroke of genius!"

When the credits listed are minimal, the submission made is usually for a small part, such as a day player. It is up to the actor to do well in all auditions in order to be considered for a featured or lead part. Established casting directors will usually only see union actors.

Community theatre, Off-Off-Broadway, student films, and most non-union projects don't employ a casting director due to limited funds. The director usually conducts the auditions.

However, at professional auditions there is that "gatekeeper" to get past. That is what this book is all about.

I will teach you how to overcome the audition problems casting directors complain about and I'll pass on to you their advice. I will tell you how to correct every mistake you might have already made. You will learn how to avoid making these mistakes in order for you to get the callback and succeed at it, to own the part, and to hear those magic words directed to *you*, "You got the part!"

1.

HOW TO GET
THE AUDITION

SEVERAL TIMES EACH AND EVERY WEEK, YEAR AFTER YEAR, I am asked by acting students how to get an audition. There are very important steps you must take in order to present the best of who you are as an actor—first to agents, and then to casting directors. Casting directors are, after all, waiting to see you if you have something to offer them. If you are reading these words, you *do* have something to offer them already: the desire to act, the desire to learn! You have taken the first step.

The next step after the desire is training. Perhaps you have had training and are embarking on the adventure of learning the art of auditioning, and it *is* an art. Auditioning is acting; however, there is no such thing as character development in the cold (prepared) reading audition. After all, you are not given the entire script to read through. You don't rehearse; you prepare, which is quite different from a rehearsal process.

For professional theatre, rehearsals are several hours a day, at least five times a week, over a period of four to twelve weeks or even more. The entire script is yours to work on. You get off book (memorize), rehearse with the ensemble (the cast), make mistakes and correct them, and grow into

the character. You are being directed. None of these elements exists in the cold reading. You prepare for the cold
reading with one or perhaps a few pages from the scene,
which are called the *sides;* they are given to you immediately before the audition or hopefully an hour or a day in
advance. You don't get off book; you don't go over the sides
with anyone; and there is no director working with you.

The rehearsal schedule for film differs in that most
directors don't hold lengthy rehearsals; instead, a perfuncto-
ry rehearsal is held before each scene. There are film directors, however, known as "actors' directors" (the best kind),
who rehearse the cast at least two weeks prior to the shoot.

In the monologue audition, you get off book and
rehearse the piece until it is ready to be performed at the
audition. Many agents, when interviewing you, will require
one or two monologues to audition you; others want a cold
reading. Theatre casting directors, for the most part, request
monologues as your first audition; the cold reading is the
callback.

Casting directors will not grant auditions to those with
no training, experience, and, in virtually all cases, with no
representation by an agent.

WHAT KIND OF TRAINING DO YOU NEED?

I teach a course entitled Acting for the Audition. It covers
theatre, film, and television. Several times each week, I
receive phone calls from potential students with no previous
training who say they want to take my Acting for the
Audition course, have their headshots taken as soon as possible (in some cases they have *already* had their headshots
taken), and get right out there to "choose" an agent! This is
an unrealistic approach to pursuing a career as a professional actor. First of all, beginning actors do not have the luxury
of choosing agents—they audition and hope to be chosen.
Secondly, there is very little chance that they will get any-

where without investing time and effort in the critical activity of training!

Acting is skilled labor and as New York casting director Stuart Howard puts it, "You can't wing it." A solid basic technique class should be the first course taken. In college drama programs, this class is always the first one given. If you are not enrolled in a college drama program and are planning to study with professional acting teachers, find one who teaches this course, which might be given in two parts: basic technique 1 and then basic technique 2. Take them both! These classes are probably the most important acting classes you will ever take. It is in these programs that you will be given a solid foundation to draw upon when you graduate to more advanced classes and when you are auditioning, rehearsing, and performing.

Next come scene study classes which will enable you to create inner-life choices for your characters, to master skills in script interpretation, to become adept at character analysis, rehearsal technique, ensemble acting, and the actor/ director relationship. In some courses, you will be given the opportunity to perform before a live audience, a highly beneficial experience for a student of acting (although you will *always* be learning your craft throughout your *entire* career).

Voice and speech classes are important because I find that very few students have adequate breath control, excellent diction, and proper vocal projection.

Your body is your instrument as is your voice and it must be disciplined, strong, and working for you. It behooves you to take classes in body movement, fencing, or dance. Each and every character you will ever play has his or her own body language, and you will need to be aware of your own body and its expressive possibilities in order to take on a character's physicality.

For musical work, of course singing classes are vital and sight-reading is a must.

On-camera classes, for the most part, focus on the technical, getting acquainted with the camera, and hopefully learning to be at ease with it. If you take such a class, it should *not* be at the expense of relinquishing in-depth acting classes.

Soap opera classes are also technical, offering sides from scripts that do not reflect true dramatic literature. If your goal is to do soap opera, again, please take in-depth acting classes first. Although most soap actors are cast by type, not talent (beauty, more than talent, is of the utmost importance for most of the characters), you still have to show that you have had acting training on your résumé, and a decent audition is expected.

A how-to-audition course will then take you to the next but perhaps not final step; many working actors return to take a brush-up course. The guidelines for scene study and rehearsal technique differ from those of acting for the audition, but they are complementary. The results expected by the casting director at the audition and the director during rehearsals are the same, although the process of getting there differs. If adequate classes have been taken, the class in auditioning will help you to pull it all together and prepare you for the most difficult area of this business: the audition!

Your Headshot and Résumé

At the completion of training (and not before) you should be doing research on finding a top-notch photographer who specializes in actors' headshots. Get referrals and interview a few in their studios. Look at their portfolios and determine how you feel about the pictures you are viewing. Ask actors to show you their photos and then decide if you feel that the photographer did well by that actor.

The headshot should look exactly like you currently look—only better! We've got to recognize you when you show up for your appointment.

Choose black as the color of your upper clothing so that your face is the focal point. Wearing white draws our eye to that item of clothing first. Don't wear a pattern; keep it simple. Wear daytime clothing rather than fancy evening wear. Jackets are flattering on men, but a well-made black shirt is fine.

If you are blond, the background should be dark gray or black, and if your hair is dark, the background should be off-white. At least one of the shots chosen should show teeth, especially if you have good ones. For commercials, good teeth are essential even for those not dealing with dental products.

Headshots mean exactly that: headshots. There is no need to have a picture of your body below the chest. Your height and weight will be listed on your résumé attached to the picture. On the other hand, the picture should not be from the neck up; then it becomes an "in your face" picture. It's very uncomfortable to view all that face spread over the entire shot!

Women should be professionally made up by the photographer's makeup person if they are not adept at applying black and white photography makeup. The makeup person or stylist will help you with your hair also.

Men with light lashes could use a very small amount of eyeliner on the lower lid to help accent the eyes. A small amount of dark eye shadow can be applied to the upper lid to accent the eyes. Normally, however, makeup is not necessary for men.

Do not wear any large jewelry. Small earrings and/or a thin chain will suffice. Men should not wear jewelry. Casting directors don't want to see you adorned with metals or stones.

You should not require more than two shots, but go ahead and indulge yourself if there are many wonderful ones and if your budget allows. Agents don't mind having more than two. They pick, choose, and send the casting director the one that best represents the character they will be submitting you for. Be aware, however, that this can be costly to you, especially if your agent doesn't subscribe to the service that allows the casting director to return your picture if you are rejected.

Please do not hire the photographer on the basis of price. Those who wind up having to have new pictures taken spend more in the long run than if they had gone to a highly recommended photographer. All the first-rate photographers charge about the same, give or take a few dollars. A good headshot should last at least five years unless you drastically change your appearance or if you are a teenager, in which case you are in the process of physically maturing. You might need a new headshot in three or four years.

I look at headshots every day. When one comes before me representing an actor I know, and it appears in the shot that the actor looks much older, I advise the actor to put the picture away and use it five to ten years into the future (that is, if the actor *still* needs to audition by then!) Unfortunately, this occurs too often; but only when photographers don't take the time to study your face, bone structure, and expressions to determine the proper lighting for you.

When you choose your shots have them reproduced in a matte finish. The glossy finish is very 1950s and is all right if you are singing in a nightclub. Your photographer will reproduce your pictures or you will send them to a reproduction laboratory recommended by the photographer.

You will need about fifty copies of each shot. If you already have an agent interested in you, you might want to bring the contact sheets (sheets of photographic paper containing miniature prints from all the negatives) to the agent, who will advise you which pictures he or she thinks are the best to print.

Staple your picture to your résumé with picture and résumé facing out. The first line on the résumé should have your name (very large if there is little to put on the résumé; the more credits you get, the smaller your name can be). The second line should state your phone number. When you obtain an agent, the agency's logo and telephone number will replace yours. Don't list your address for two reasons. At this point, all communication is done by phone; your agent is the only one who needs your address. Also, you don't know whose hands your headshot might fall into and you don't want just anyone to know where you live!

On the third line, put your union status, if you are a member. The fourth line is your height, weight, hair, eye color, and, if you so wish, your age range, which is a ten-year span. In this business you are as old as you *look,* not as old as you *are.*

If you have done film and/or TV work, the next line is your first heading: FILM/TV. List any camera work you might have done, including the name of your character, the name of the project, and the name of the production company. If you have not done any camera work, eliminate this heading. The next heading is THEATRE; use the same format as above. Include theatre credits from college if there were performances for an audience, summer camp, and, if recently out of high school, include those productions. Don't despair if there is little or nothing so far that you can enter on the résumé. The first résumé of *all* of us is very little more than a blank piece of paper.

Now put the heading, REPRESENTATIVE ROLES. List all the credits you have performed in scenes from your acting classes. Give the names of the characters, and the names of the plays. Name the workshops you performed the scenes in. If they all were performed in one workshop, list the name on the same line as the heading. This category, first and foremost, puts words on the résumé, and it enables the agent and casting director to see the types of characters you were cast in by your teacher(s), some of whom, like me, are casting directors. This is not a falsification of credits; it is not stated that you performed these parts in plays in a theatre. We might embellish slightly on a résumé but we must not lie.

The next heading is TRAINING. Put the list of teachers you have trained with, including degrees from college drama programs. Omit training in any other field of endeavor. This is an actor's résumé. We don't care if you have studied archeology.

The next heading is SPECIAL SKILLS. Casting directors are not interested in the hobbies and interests that some actors are wont to state under this heading; they only want to know about the activities that you are adept in, such as sports; list each one. State musical instruments you play (if any), if you are a good dancer (what kind of dance), and if you can sing (what is the voice range and what kind of music). Listing your musical talents in the special skills category shows that you are an actor who can sing and dance, not a singer and dancer who can act. If, on the other hand, your goal is to audition for musicals, then, under your name, state your voice range and/or dance discipline (all Broadway musicals hire dancers with ballet training). If you love animals, list that you are "great with animals;" same thing for children. The special skills category is to display what physical activities you can provide as needed for commercials and shows that you are not afraid of or allergic to animals, are familiar with kids, and so on.

The next heading is ACCENTS/DIALECTS/FOREIGN LANGUAGE. If an accent is required for the character, your agent should provide this information to you at least two days prior to your audition appointment. This information is listed in the character breakdown sent by the casting director. (The process of learning an accent is covered in chapter 12.)

List a few accents on the résumé, such as standard English, cockney, southern American, Noo Yawkese, Irish, etc. Choose the ones you feel you do well enough with a one- or two-day preparation. At the end of this list, include "with a twenty-four- (or forty-eight-, if you think two days is necessary) hour notice."

If you speak foreign languages, list them. If fluent, say so. If you don't speak a foreign language, omit the words "foreign language" from the heading.

This is a basic professional acting résumé. A mainstream agent should be qualified to assist you with your résumé. I find that most of the lower echelon agents know little or nothing about the proper résumé format. I have redone several that have come before me that were totally unacceptable.

AGENTS AND HOW TO GET ONE

The next step is getting an agent. Finding one who wants to represent you is a very frustrating experience. Mainstream agents have a full roster of every type and age range of actors. Chances are if you feel the need to switch agents or upgrade your representation and you already have a "money" résumé—meaning you are a film/television union member and have done featured, lead parts or commercials—agents will be interested in you. But if you are starting out with more white on the page than black, they will be hesitant to represent you—*unless* you have what I call the "hair-teeth-and-bone-structure-school-of-acting face." Agents on both coasts and in Toronto have told me that if I had any student with "that" kind of face, the kind that, as more than one has said, "would stop traffic because of the beauty, send them right over!" These individuals, having no concern with talent, will be hired by type. (I teach how to be hired for talent.)

There is virtually no acting challenge in auditioning for and doing an SOC (silent on camera) part or a day player with five or less lines. These parts are usually cast by type.

If you are not a union member I recommend that you do not send your picture and résumé to the top level agents who represent stars only. Mail or bring them to all the others; if that sounds overwhelming, send ten at a time. Give the agents at least two weeks to respond by phone or by returning your picture. Chances are if they haven't by then, they probably aren't planning to contact you for an appointment, although it has happened that an agent's response was a month or two later. Include a SASE (self-addressed, stamped envelope)—if you don't, they will discard your picture. Having more pictures reproduced can be expensive, but do not send laser copies, which admittedly are much cheaper to reproduce, because the auditors dislike them; most lasers are very flattering and often don't represent you accurately.

Also included should be a short cover letter saying:

Dear (name of agent),

Enclosed is my picture and résumé for your perusal. I would like to have the opportunity to audition for you in the very near future. Thank you for your consideration. I look forward to hearing from you.

Sincerely,

(your name)

Write no more than these words. Your résumé speaks for itself and agents don't have the time to read a lengthy dissertation. Hopefully, some agents might respond and set up an appointment with you. If so, be prepared to do a monologue or two and/or a cold reading for them. Wear your most beautiful daytime outfit and leave off the perfume or cologne. In chapter 4, you'll see what Los Angeles, *Everybody Loves Raymond* casting director Lisa Miller Katz has to say about scents in her office!

Your appointment with the agent is not just for the audition; it is also an interview. In an interview *you are your own audition!* At a properly conducted interview, you should not be asked what your experience is; it is on the résumé. However, do not be surprised if the agent looks over your résumé, puts it down, and says to you, "So tell me what your experience is as an actor." You might be tempted to look at him like he's crazy, but please resist doing so. Just talk about what you have done as brightly and pleasantly as you can, as if the résumé was not right on the desk. Many agents do not know how to conduct an interview. The two of you should be talking about everything except what is on the résumé. You might, of course, be asked what the experience was like for you working with a certain director or teacher or so forth listed on the résumé. Be positive about all you relate. Omit any negative statements regarding your experiences. Make an impression that you are an outgoing, optimistic, easygoing person.

You are being observed as you talk. The agent is looking at your facial expressions, body language, and your eye appeal to determine if you are likable and if you impart audience appeal for camera and theatre. This is, you see, an audition! Be prepared to do your monologue(s) and the reading, the second half of your audition. The audition will take place right there in the agent's office, which in virtually all cases is a small room, or it will take place in a special room used for meetings and auditions; the dimensions of such a room are about the size of the average living room. Other agents in the organization might be invited in to view your audition.

At the conclusion of the interview/audition, many agents will tell you that they need to see more of your work before making a decision. You are instructed to send a flyer of the next production you are in. What the agent is saying is, your work that day wasn't strong enough or appealing enough to be granted representation. The agent who bluntly critiques your work is doing you a favor, but some are not capable of offering constructive acting counsel. Think about what you did and be realistic as to whether you are ready for an agent or if more training is necessary. Be brutally honest; it's for your benefit.

Eventually, if you have ample training, a great picture, and do a good job in your interview/audition with an agent, you will secure representation.

You will be given a form to fill out requiring you to state all vital statistics regarding clothing sizes and measurements: dress, suit, shirt, neck, inseam, glove, hat, shoes, bra, etc.

Some (not all) agents will want you to sign a contract for a year. If you feel comfortable with the agent, sign, but *please read the entire contract before signing!* If, by the end of the year, you have not been cast from the several auditions you have been set up for, chances are the agent will not renew the contract; you will get a pleasant letter of termination.

Agents who don't require a contract still expect you to honor all appointments made for you by them. Also, if you happen to get a paying part on your own (highly improbable, but it can happen if you know someone in the production), they expect you to disclose all information to them, allowing them to negotiate so they can get their 15 percent commission. My feeling is either you have an agent or you don't! If you are in an area where freelancing is acceptable, hopefully you are the client of more than one agent and, of course, whoever submits you receives the commission.

I once got an audition through my friend's agent, who called me to find out where her client was. When I informed her that her client was far away on vacation (she should have informed her agent of her plans), the agent said, "Well, why don't you go in her place!" I said I would because I knew my friend would not be able to get back in time. Her agent called the casting director to change the name from her client to mine. She gave me all the information regarding the project, where to go, and when. I thanked her (if I got the part she would share in the commission). When I hung up I first left a message on the casting director's machine stating who represented me. Then I called my agent and passed on what just transpired. I was a little piqued that my own agent didn't submit me for the part but I let it go. I got the callback and the part. My friend was not upset with me; she had decided (as I knew) that she wouldn't have come back for the audition; she was having a wonderful time where she was. We are still the best of friends.

The more revenue you bring into the office, the brighter the agent's smile will be toward you. The success of the agency depends on your success at the auditions.

GETTING AUDITION APPOINTMENTS

Casting directors don't want you to call them or drop into their offices; they resent this. Casting directors only see actors by appointments that are initiated with agents. They say you are wasting your time and some of them have actually stated to me that you are annoying them. It is your agent you should be sending postcards to and visiting if they have not been in touch with you for a while.

This statement represents the attitudes of virtually all North American casting directors. This is not rudeness (although it may appear to be to you) on their part; it is professionalism.

An agent submits pictures and résumés to casting directors upon taking on a new client and again as the breakdowns arrive daily on the agent's fax. The breakdown, compiled by the casting director, states the description of the characters. If you fit into the description, your agent will submit you for the part. An agent cannot *get* you an audition; they can only *submit* you. The casting director grants you the audition. The director *hires* you. The producer *pays* you. The audience *loves* you.

These are the steps to getting an audition. The remainder of these pages will give you the tools to succeed at the audition. Throughout these chapters casting directors offer their comments on what constitutes a winning audition.

2.

AUDITION/INTERVIEW ETIQUETTE

IT IS IMPORTANT FOR ACTORS TO REMEMBER THAT WHEN THEY walk into an audition or interview they are candidates for a job. Because acting is an artistic, highly competitive, and uncommon form of employment requiring rather unusual talents and skills, actors may sometimes lack knowledge of, or forget, some of the rules of professional conduct and courtesy.

At first glance, some of the suggestions in this chapter may seem like commonsensical advice that any job seeker would follow. But since, on a daily basis, so many casting directors see actors engaged in self-sabotaging behavior, it is very important that you read and follow the advice herein.

BEING LATE

Each casting director interviewed commented on how lateness causes problems for them at the audition. The following is a summary of the comments.

JUDY HENDERSON

It appears that most actors who are late are the young ones! Don't wait until you reach a certain age to finally become a responsible person. You have a responsibility to yourself and an obligation to us to be on time. Take your career seriously; don't be late.

LEONARD FINGER
Don't come into the audition late or exhausted due to personal problems.

LIZ RAMOS
Being late causes stress. If you do come late please do not apologize over and over. Once is enough.

JANN STEFOFF
Don't be late. It sounds simple, but being on time is an extremely important issue around here. Sometimes we schedule performers to work with other actors, and being late can lessen those other performers' chances of doing a decent audition. If you arrive late please don't demand to be taken out of turn and don't announce that you have to leave if you're not brought in right away. This bugs the hell out of us.

CHRISTY L. POKARNEY
Don't come in rushed with a lack of focus in an unprofessional manner.

All the casting directors agreed on the following:
Being on time exhibits a professional behavior. We are looking forward to our appointment with you and we truly want you to succeed. Being late causes you stress which can have an adverse effect on your performance. You might have personal problems causing you to be late and we sympathize with you, but we have a job to do and we actually need you to help us do our job well. Have respect for your fellow actors who did arrive on time.

Are you one of those people who can't seem to arrive on time for appointments? It's bad enough when you keep friends waiting; it is resented by all who are at the designated place at the precise time prearranged and then must wait for you.

If you are late for a business appointment, job interview, or audition, surely you must know what your tardiness indicates. You are not a reliable, well-organized person, and therefore cannot be trusted. If you were to be part of the organization or production, it would be assumed that you would upset the regimen. Your lateness affects those around you and sabotages the proceedings.

If you are late for your audition, you'd better give an extraordinary reading in order to compensate for your late-ness—that is, *if* you are allowed to audition. You might just be sent on your way and not be given another appointment. The auditors endeavor in every way to adhere to their sched-ule. If you are late for rehearsals, you will be yelled at, fined, and/or fired. For film, you can't afford to be late until you become a major star and reap millions of dollars for the stu-dio, and even then there are directors who will refuse to work with you.

You should always leave in plenty of time in the event of a subway breakdown, an accident on the road holding up traffic, inclement weather, or the possibility of some cata-strophic event along the way. It is advisable to get there too early rather than arrive late. Go to a juice bar and indulge in a brain and immune-system enhancing drink. Go to a natur-al food store or market and get a bottle of juice or water. Take a relaxing walk. Do creative visualization exercises. Meditate. All the aforementioned are valuable to your prepa-ration and performance.

Arrive at the place of audition at least one half hour before your appointment in order to prepare.

The auditors resent lateness. They have a schedule to adhere to as best as they can. They don't want the audition-ee upsetting their routine. You have points against you immediately and the casting director and director know you arrived late. All the auditors have a sheet of paper which lists the time of the actors' appointed time slots. They are not interested in your excuses and your personal problems. You are going to have personal problems when you are performing in the production. These problems belong off the stage, outside of the soundstage, off the lot, and out of the casting director's office.

If you are late you will (at least you should) be stressed out because of your tardiness and this condition will affect your preparation and performance.

Take into account the importance of the audition and how much you want the part. You've spent a sizable amount of money on training, headshots, résumés, and proper clothing in preparation for the career you have chosen. Don't blow it all by indulging in a very sloppy habit, an indifferent attitude, or getting stressed-out because you're late.

Be professional. Be on time.

I have a friend who is habitually late. She has no concept of time, gets involved in minute things instead of getting ready, doesn't know how to cut a phone call short, and therefore arrives for appointments anywhere from a half hour to over an hour late. I retain her friendship because when she finally does show up, she is a source of incredible fun, laughter, adventure, and positivity; she is imbued with a spirit of generosity. Her habitual and very annoying lateness is inconsistent with her highly enjoyable company.

I no longer meet her where I must stand in a theatre lobby or sit at a table in a restaurant while waiting for her. If we have plans to go to the theatre, I make sure she has her ticket. She arrives after the first act, where I have been ensconced in my seat well in advance of the beginning of act one in order to read the entire playbill. At the movies, I buy my ticket and go in to ensure myself of a seat halfway down and in the middle, saving the one next to me. I refuse to tell her what she has missed until we are on our way out of the theatre or movie house.

If we meet at my place I tell her to be an hour earlier than I actually want her to show up. She still arrives an hour late but it is the actual time that I expect her.

I have talked to her about this problem several times. I told her that by making people wait for her, she is in essence saying, "Screw you! I don't give a damn that you have to wait for me!" Actually my words were stated in a much stronger way, not appropriate for these pages.

I have done some analyzing regarding her lateness, but due to the fact that I hold no proper degree in psychiatry (just the homegrown kind), I will spare you my conclusions.

This person is an actor! She swears that she is on time for her auditions. She has been hired for some parts, but, as far as I am concerned, not enough considering her vast talents and wonderful physical type. I wonder if, indeed, she is really on time for them.

CANCELING YOUR APPOINTMENT

There are a few legitimate reasons why an actor should cancel the audition appointment; being sick is one of them. Any catastrophic event in your life merits a cancellation. However, one casting director believes illness does not merit a cancellation.

STEPHANIE GORIN
We all have to work when we're sick or even in not the best of moods and you just try to do your best.

The other casting directors were of another opinion.
Although we admire the sick actor who doesn't want to miss the audition, please don't come to the audition sneezing and coughing. Chances are you won't give a winning performance if you are really feeling awful. Call in sick and ask to be rescheduled. We get sick too and we will gladly do our best to accommodate you. If the office is small you will be spreading your germs around. Stay home. Get well.

I feel that it is absolutely reasonable to cancel an audition due to an illness that renders you feverish, weak, nauseous, and completely out of sorts (unless you have an appointment with Ms. Gorin, who, by the way, not only is highly respected for her professionalism but is also quite a lovely, sympathetic lady who really would *not* want you to compromise your health). Under these circumstances call or have someone call your agent or the casting director; it is imperative that the message gets through *before* your scheduled appointment.

I know how badly you want to keep your appointment even though you are ill, but I also know how much everyone at the casting office will resent you for spreading your germs amongst them.

I counsel my students that, as actors, they can't afford to become ill. I tell them to ensure that their immune systems are not compromised, by eating properly (no fast food, no sugar, no meat consumption or very little), taking an abundance of the right supplements (including Echinacea, the immune booster), keeping stress at the lowest level possible (and doing relaxation exercises daily), getting enough sleep, not smoking, keeping the booze intake at a minimum, drinking a lot of distilled water, thinking positively, and removing anyone from their lives who is not enhancing their lives (get out of that rotten relationship—*now*).

Don't go to the audition when you are more than moderately sick. Call and ask for another appointment. Hopefully they can accommodate you. If not, I believe your health and welfare should be your priority.

Waiting Room Do's and Don't's

The casting directors were in agreement regarding waiting room behavior.

Leonard Finger

Don't get testy with the assistant/secretary in the outer office.

LOUISE MACKIEWICZ

Please be pleasant and treat the monitor, assistant, or secretary in the outer office with respect. This person is a very close associate and we discuss everything. Don't have an inappropriate conversation in the waiting area, for instance, bad-mouthing the product or being insensitive when children are around. Please make sure all your sizes are filled in the casting sheet. This is an additional phone call we have to make if you get the job.

JULI-ANN KAY

As you are accompanied from the waiting room into the audition room do not only look for the casting director or director but pay attention to the person bringing you in who is probably an associate casting director or assistant to the director.

LIZ RAMOS

Don't talk to friends in the waiting room; it could cost you the job. Spend the time to get right in your body. If you do talk please keep your voice down.

CATHY WESELUCK

Some actors appear to squander their focusing energies by socializing with other actors too much in the waiting area and seem scattered because of not taking enough time to settle into their role when asked to begin.

The casting directors agreed on the following:
It is best for all if you don't bring a child or a dog to the audition. Children make noise and they don't like to be made to sit still. However, if you must, of course bring them. After all, we all love children. Dogs can be distracting in many ways because of possible behavior problems. We feel that dogs would feel comfortable if left in their own environment (even though we love them). If you must bring them, they should be small, quiet, and well behaved.

Please don't complain that you had to wait too long. Every effort is made to honor all appointments on time but events occur that can cause the proceedings to run late. Make sure to be right there when your name is called. Please turn off your cell phones when you arrive. You should be preparing for the audition, not talking to someone, not to mention how distracting it is for those around you who are preparing.

I think the most important advice I can give to young people (and old) is, "Be kind to each other." It sounds so simple but there is a lack of kindness in this world. Love affairs, marriages, friendships, and world peace would thrive, perhaps forever, if only kindness was practiced each and every day. It is very difficult to turn away from one who displays kindness.

This applies to those who are not necessarily the principal people in our life. Each and every person you encounter in the work world and in social events deserves to be treated civilly.

Why, then, do actors not exhibit respect to monitors at the audition? Do they feel superior? If one *feels* superior, one is *not!*

Is it that they are overwrought by the fact that in a few minutes they will be put on display? If you are well-trained and well-prepared for the audition, you will not be overwrought! There is never an excuse for bad behavior under these circumstances.

You are being observed in the waiting area. In essence, the audition has begun. There are several ways in which to sabotage yourself before you enter the audition room.

Unfortunately it appears that in human nature, there are those who will only show respect and exhibit courteous behavior to individuals in a position of power. Too many actors operate on the assumption that the monitor greeting the actor in the waiting area and accompanying him or her into the audition room is nothing more than a very minor player whose stature in the production is nil. Be advised that this person is representing the production and therefore *is* in a position of power. He or she will apprise the casting director of an auditionee's behavior. It's a pity that *all* living beings are not treated with equal respect.

STICKING TO THE SCHEDULE

Be prepared to be taken in at the scheduled time of your appointment. One should not have the audacity to demand to be taken out of turn! This kind of behavior is unacceptable. It displays a lack of humanity on the part of the actor. You are not in the position to make demands.

It's true that at times you will be called in before your scheduled time, and this can be disconcerting. You've assiduously planned your schedule to get there in ample time to prepare and suddenly your name is called. I understand your frustration and annoyance but you must not allow this situation to sabotage your performance. Stay as calm as possible. You might gently mention to the monitor that your appointment is not for another thirty minutes and then you may ask if it would be possible to be given just a few minutes more to prepare. You will get a yes or no. If it is a no, pull all your dignity together and go forth, perhaps incorporating into the scene that you, as the character, would have liked to have more time to think this situation out.

You may also convey to the casting director when you get into the audition room or on the stage, that what you are about to do amounts to an ice-cold reading. Explain (in as short a time as possible) the situation. It is very possible that the casting director didn't realize that you were called in before your scheduled appointment and just might grant you more time to prepare. Sometimes, it is the monitor who shifts things around to ensure finishing on time or often earlier; or the monitor doesn't want to work overtime. As much as you might not believe it, you do have rights.

On the other hand, auditions sometimes run late. It is possible that your name might not be called at the precise time of your scheduled appointment.

Space your appointments to cover yourself. Assume you will have to wait and in the event that this occurs, please do not complain to the monitor.

You certainly have the right to communicate to this person (in the nicest way) that you have another appointment and must not be late. Ask if you can be rescheduled if this is the case. However, as I said, give yourself plenty of time between appointments and just sit patiently (doing your preparation) until you are called.

And sometimes it is the disappearing actors who throw the auditions off schedule. Where are you when your name is being called? Why is it that so many actors are in the bathroom or out in the hall or putting change in the parking meter or making a phone call or—heaven forbid—outside grabbing a smoke?

It is okay—in fact, advisable—to keep away from any activity to ensure quiet while you are preparing. I have prepared in the hallway, the stairwell, or even outside on the sidewalk to isolate myself from any type of noise, specifically talking. But at the approximate time of your appointment, you must make sure you are right there in the waiting room. If not, you just might forfeit your audition if your name is called and there is no response.

WAITING ROOM CONVERSATIONS

Have a sense of propriety in the waiting room. If you indulge in any kind of conversation (which you should not be doing—you should be staying in character and continuously preparing) keep it quiet, end it swiftly, and have some decorum. Others are preparing for their reading and there might be children there who are auditioning.

I am appalled on the streets and in the subway when I hear people (usually teenagers showing off how "mature" they are) conversing with obscenities at a volume high enough for all within one hundred feet to be subjected to.

This kind of behavior reflects a lack of self-respect; if you respect yourself you will respect others.

My students know only too well that I am far from being prudish with my language, but I instinctively know when, to whom, and where I may indulge in four letter words. Certainly, the waiting area at the casting director's office is off-limits to such language and behavior. Your reading would have to be extremely brilliant to compensate for bad behavior, and even then, I have seen directors take an actor's picture out of the callback pile when informed by the monitor of undesirable behavior. Bad behavior cancels out a good reading.

When auditioning for a commercial, what would possess you to bad-mouth the product? If you think poorly of the product, do not audition. Or, once there, think positively about why you are there, and even if it is a product that you dislike, for whatever reason, find some redeeming quality about it.

I would have a problem with auditioning for a product manufactured by a company that conducted laboratory experiments on animals. I would not go to such an audition. I once had a soup commercial where I was told I would have to eat the soup as part of the audition. I could not attain information in advance if the soup used for the audition would be vegetarian and I worried and fretted over how I would handle the dilemma. As it turned out, they did choose vegetarian soup for us to taste, much to my relief.

STAYING FOCUSED

It's only natural to look around to see if you recognize a working actor in the waiting area or if there is anyone there you know. If you spot an actor whom you've seen in several commercials or productions and who is now auditioning for the same part you are auditioning for, more likely than not your thoughts are something like, "He or she's going to get this, not me." This is self-defeating. You have just as good a chance as the working actor.

It's true that one who has been hired multiple times is, first and foremost, auditioning very well, is also the right type being sought each time, and has proven to be reliable and professional in every way. However, the auditors are always looking for a fresh face. They love to make discoveries. That working actor wasn't always a working actor.

If you spend that valuable time in the waiting area by diligently preparing and concentrating on you, as character, you will be a strong contender for the part. And as you are deeply involved in your preparation, someone there is being intimidated by you!

FILLING OUT THE PAPERWORK

When you audition for camera work, you will be given a casting sheet to fill out in the waiting room. It is a sheet of paper stating the shoot dates and asking for your availability on those days. You are also asked for your vital statistics including your height, weight, measurements, clothing, shoe size, etc. The casting director wants this information on hand in the event that you will be hired for the job, at which time the list will be given to the wardrobe department. If you don't fill it out the day of your audition in the waiting area and you get hired, the process is slowed down because they don't have this information on hand.

SMALL DOGS AND BABIES

Regarding bringing your child or dog to the audition, you will probably cause a problem in the waiting room and during the audition. If there was no casting call for children, there should be none there. However, if you cannot get a baby-sitter and you are certain that your child will sit in a seat and not utter a sound, bring him or her. As a mother of three, I would have never had the assurance under these circumstances, that any of mine would be silent and stay put. This goes against the very nature of children (or at least mine). Obviously you don't want to relinquish the opportunity to audition and you can't leave your child unattended. The monitor is not a baby-sitter; that person is on the job working hard on behalf of the production.

The only time I have ever seen a child at the audition where we were accepting of the situation was when the actor was a very established working actor with whom we were familiar and for whom we had a lot of affection. She brought the child into the audition room. We put up with the intrusion. Just once!

As for bringing a dog, let me first assure you that *no one* loves dogs (or any kind of animal) as much as I do, or at least more than I. I would love to *always* be accompanied by my animals. But there are people who have allergies, and many are afraid of dogs. If your dog is more than seven pounds, I must advise you to leave it at home. However, under seven pounds, dogs can be carried in a pouch by you, like an infant, with just their little heads showing. The best pouch on the market is called The Pee-Ka-Boo Pouch that tiny dogs love to be in, manufactured by Munroe Enterprises LLC, *janico99@aol.com*. Or you can place your little one within a large canvas handbag that you carry on your shoulder. No one at the casting session need know that there is a dog within their midst if it is in the shoulder bag (hopefully no one is allergic to dogs). You can put the pouch or bag on the floor near you while you are doing your reading. It is important for your dog to know that there is to be no barking, crying, or walking out of the pouch or bag. If you have the dog in the pouch, of course the casting director will notice its presence. If you've brought the dog in the bag, its face might appear and some or all of the auditors will probably be enraptured and make a fuss (most auditors actually *do* love dogs). They might, on the other hand, be upset upon discovering that the dog was there all along. With the pouch, they know of its presence from the onset. This is a chance you will have to take. I know people who use the bags for their teacup-sized dogs and they are able to take them everywhere: theatre, restaurants, hotels; and their presence is never discovered. There are many good hotels that allow dogs, so one doesn't have to hide them in those situations. The pouch is great for carrying dogs when there is no reason to hide them.

I have a very good friend who owns a teacup-sized dog. We went to the theatre together with Spud in her large shoulder bag. Once in our seats, dead center in the third row, she put him on her lap, covering him with her program. As the play was about to begin I suddenly remembered something she had told me about him. The only time he barks is when someone knocks on the door. I panicked as I realized that in the play we were about to see (I had seen a previous production), there are two times when characters knock on the door! I frantically whispered this to her. She whispered back that I should alert her when those two knocks would be occurring and she would put her hands over his ears. I told her that I sort of knew when the knocks would be but I didn't know if I could alert her in time. She kept her hands poised ready to block his hearing and I managed to alert her in time. Until then, I was a nervous wreck.

ELECTRONIC ETIQUETTE

I will counsel you as I do my students when they arrive for their classes with me; turn off your cell phones and pagers and keep them off until you have vacated the premises!

Having your cell phone or pager ring while in the waiting area or the audition room is blatantly intrusive! It is rude to carry on a conversation on the phone in the waiting room as others near you are preparing for their auditions, as you should be doing. The waiting area is to be as quiet as possible. If the ring or a beep is heard during the audition, it is a blatant intrusion on the proceedings. The casting director and all the auditors will be perturbed. You certainly don't want to create an atmosphere of hostility toward yourself.

Rudeness to Other Actors

Don't be rude to your fellow actors. If rudeness in an actor is observed by the casting director or the monitor, this behavior is a sure sign that you will continue to be rude to your fellow actors during the production. This infraction at the audition can disqualify you from a production. All the casting directors concurred with the following statement:

> You should be courteous to your fellow actors at the audition and certainly to the reader.

You might read with another actor who is up for the other part in the scene. If you are rude to this person and the casting director notices this, chances are, no matter how good your reading might be, you will not be wanted for the project. If anyone else notices your rudeness, it will be reported to the casting director or the director. No director wants to start off a relationship with an actor who, at the onset, displays rudeness to *anyone*.

I realize that you are competing with your fellow actors who are auditioning for the same part as you are. It is natural to hope and pray that you will give a much better reading than any of them, and the part will be offered to you. Well, just make sure that you *do* give more; there is nothing immoral in going for the gold. So much in life is competing.

The actor reading with you is auditioning for the other character in the scene with you. You and he or she are a team, relying on each other. There should be good chemistry between the two of you. Therefore, it is imperative that your behavior toward this person be highly civil.

In some cases, the actor will have been hired to be a reader; that is, to read with the auditionees. Often it is not the casting director or an assistant who reads with you. Be as pleasant to this person as you would be toward the casting director. The reader is on *their* team; you are not! Yet!

It might be difficult to believe that an actor would actually be rude under these circumstances but it is true! I've been witness to this at casting sessions I have conducted. I suppose that the actor is, in a subliminal way, communicating, "Don't hire me for this or any future part." We won't!

3.
PRACTICAL PREPARATION

YOUR TALENT AND YOUR SKILLS MAY BE THE TOOLS THAT GET you the job, but the first impression you make is very important. You want to make sure that the "package" you present is an attractive one, and that includes your attire, your attitude, your headshot, and your résumé. Read on to find out how to prepare and present the most "hirable" you!

DRESSING THE PART

Actors who don't do their homework regarding the cultural and economic background of the character they are auditioning for too often dress in a most inappropriate way. Our clothing says so much about us and many actors are aware of this and yet they neglect to do the research when it comes to the audition.

DONALD CASE, LIZ RAMOS, JANN STEFOFF

Dress properly even for a one-line shoot. Get information from your agent. *Don't* wear an outrageous outfit. Wear the wardrobe we have instructed you to wear, not an outfit totally inappropriate for the audition and character. Wear clothing that fits well; the biggest offense is when the clothing is very tight and shows every bulge.

The character breakdown gives you some background about the character you will be auditioning for. If it is not apparent to you what he or she might be wearing, ask your agent to secure additional information such as the character's economic and cultural background, if the script is period or contemporary, what kind of work he or she does, and if the scene is a social event, in the workplace, or in the kitchen. Go to your closet and choose what you *feel* the character might be wearing.

Once my agent sent me on a commercial audition for the part of a cleaning woman. I was appalled that it had come to that (just joking) and I remarked that I was not imbued with one iota of domesticity (not a joke). Nevertheless, off I went. After all, as an actress, I must be open to play characters totally at variance with my sensibilities. I was the *only* one who didn't wear a housedress (don't own one) or an apron (don't own one), and although I am wont to wear scarves and kerchiefs around my head, on that day I didn't. Everyone else did. Indeed, some women brought a dustpan and broom! (I'm pretty sure I own those.) One of them got the part because I sure didn't. They were hiring for type and I really didn't think that I looked like an office cleaning lady, whatever that means. (That's what I kept telling myself.) Of course I was wrong. An office cleaning lady can be a woman of any age and look: an unemployed actress, model, secretary, a mother, a writer, a woman desirous of peace and tranquillity in her workplace, a woman who prefers working at night, etc. The character breakdown just said, "cleaning lady."

Don't choose to wear an outrageous outfit that makes it appear as if the clothing is auditioning. It can be very distracting unless the character is described as being outrageous; then go all out on the outfit. If you are auditioning for a military person, then do wear khaki pants and some sort of a top that could pass as part of fatigues or uniform, and wear heavy boots if you've got them. If you're supposed to be a female guest at a garden wedding, wear a flowery dress and a large hat. As a male, wear a summer suit. Display for the auditors that you are a thinking actor and you take your auditions seriously.

If you know that you will be auditioning for a high society character, why would you show up at the audition wearing jeans and a t-shirt? If the character is a truck driver, why would you choose to wear a suit and tie when you were told that the scene takes place in a truck stop during his run? I think you catch my drift. Wear what you feel the character would be wearing in that scene. The operative word here is "feel." You don't *know* what he or she is wearing. But as I've already said, look in your closet and with the information gathered by you about the character, choose the outfit. Chances are it's in your closet or you can borrow from a friend or, if you are flush, it can be bought (or rented).

It is never expected by the casting director that the actor wear an expensive outfit, just one that appears to be appropriate for the character. But it is always expected that the clothing worn is clean. If stains and dirt are visible, this sight is met with pure disgust by the casting director. It connotes disregard for oneself and others.

Somewhere along the line, many actors have been told a romantic myth about artists who transcend their careless appearance with their talent. While this legend might occasionally be justified when a paint-splattered artist generates an exquisite canvas, it is an utterly wrongheaded approach to the audition process. Remember, you *are* your instrument; you *are* the work that you are presenting. If your appearance is slovenly and unappealing, your talent will not be able to rise above its package. Your potential employers may assume that the sloppiness will spill over into other areas and not consider you for the part.

If, perchance, the sloppy actor gives an exemplary reading, the casting director will have a talk with the actor and mention the offending sight. If the actor cannot come up with a reasonable response, there will be no callback.

An unflattering fit indicates that the actor is not fastidious or stylish. And actors should be careful not to garb themselves in clothing that is too outlandish or vulgar. For example, a woman auditioning should not look like she just stepped out of a girlie magazine—unless the character breakdown indicates just that.

HAVE HEADSHOT, WILL TRAVEL

The headshot is your calling card. If a casting director doesn't know your work, he or she will decide to audition you based on the submission of your headshot (and résumé). After the audition (especially if the audition is not filmed) the picture will jog the memories of the auditors as they decide whom to call back. You want to make sure that if there is more than one auditor making decisions, that you have ample headshots. As Louise Mackiewicz puts it:

> Please come to the session with at least two copies of your current headshot and résumé. Although I have most local actors on file, additional copies will be for the producer, director, or agency. It is not my job to supply these.

Regarding headshots, my advice is, "Never leave home without one!" You never know who you might meet somewhere: a casting director, writer, director, etc. When you go to auditions, make sure to have a few of them with you. Often the casting director has only one and if there are several auditors, each of them might want one.

ATTITUDE ADJUSTMENT

In the first chapter, my fellow casting directors and I stressed the importance of courteous behavior toward potential employers (the people you are auditioning for). However, what is required goes a bit beyond observing social amenities. Remember, you work in a very creative and highly collaborative field. It makes total sense that your prospective bosses (*and* coworkers) would prefer to work with someone optimistic, agreeable, and flexible.

LIZ RAMOS

It is important to be polite and professional inside and outside the audition room. I have seen many actors get a role over another not because they are more talented but because the producer or director wants a more positive person in his company.

Do not bring any angst into the waiting area or audition room. You must communicate that you are happy to be there with them. Actors who have given fine readings have not been granted a callback when the monitor has reported a bad attitude to the casting director. Even if you feel justified in complaining about being kept waiting, for example, it will be construed as having "attitude." Not fair, you say? Life is not fair!

Realize that your attitude is something that you can work on and improve, just as you can work on and improve your acting craft. Learning and then practicing relaxation exercises before you enter the audition situation is one way you can take pressure off of yourself, thereby lessening anxiety and making yourself more open and available in the audition. Creative visualization, which I briefly describe in conjunction with preparing your audition monologue in chapter 19, can also be used to lighten your view of life, as can many other forms of exercise, therapy, etc. Finally, you want to set yourself up to be the most energized, sensitive, positive *you* you can be.

4.
BAD HABITS

THERE ARE MANY WAYS THAT A PERSON CAN TURN US OFF: A sour disposition, dishonesty, and lack of commitment to anything beyond his own instant gratification. Then there is personal hygiene. While most actors are cognizant of proper hygiene and by and large are well kempt and stylish, some of the issues surrounding personal deportment are more subtle than one might think. It is necessary to mention these few comments.

SHASTA LUTZ
Make sure your hands are clean. Bad breath or BO are guaranteed bad impressions. Sounds simple but the amount of people I've seen who neglect these standards . . . Please do not yawn in the middle of your audition, this has happened! Get a good night's sleep.

LISA MILLER KATZ
Please do not wear strong perfumes in auditions. My office is very small, and most scents remain long after the actor has left.

All agreed on the following:
Do not chew gum during an interview or reading.

We've come a long way since Elizabethan days in England when actors had to place themselves far from each other to avoid the assault of each other's stench.

There is no excuse for being unclean and practicing bad hygiene. Slovenliness is indicative of disesteem for oneself and for others. Such people inflict their lack of sanitation on others. It's actually a hostile act borne out of a past unresolved trauma. It is rare when such an actor comes before us, but obviously it does occur.

THE SCENT OF A WOMAN (OR A MAN!)

Regarding wearing strong perfume or cologne, take this very seriously. It is best to either wear a *very* small amount of a top-of-the-line scent or none at all when you know you will be auditioning in an office. There are several inexpensive perfumes and men's colognes, used by actors not able to afford the best, that deliver an odor similar to bug or bathroom spray!

Many people are allergic to perfumes. Perhaps some casting directors are allergic. Why take a chance? I don't wear perfume when I am going to be with people who suffer from allergies to perfume. I love wearing my perfume. I have two favorite scents but there are times when I must socialize or work sans perfume. Of course, you don't know in advance if this is the case when auditioning, so play it safe; go scentless or mildly and expensively scented.

SPIT OUT THE GUM

In my classes when an actor gets up to perform a scene, I can always tell if he has gum in his mouth. You really can't hide it even if you are not actually chewing it. I stop the actor and instruct him to deposit the gum in the garbage immediately. Chewing gum is an intrusion. It almost becomes another character, one who is uninvited. We are looking at your face as you talk, and even the most subtle extra movement of the mouth and surrounding muscles creates a distortion larger than life. Under these circumstances, your facial expression has no connection to the emotional life of the character.

Actors who keep gum in their mouth during an audition, by and large, have not made the choice that the character is doing the chewing. It is a very sloppy, nonthinking, amateurish indiscretion. And for those who use gum as a prop for their character, this is a very poor cliché. Use your acting powers to create the character, not props.

Your Brain Needs Oxygen

Regarding yawning during the audition, I'm surprised because when one is emotionally stimulated and in a heightened state of excitement, one usually does not yawn. Therefore, I would assume the yawning indicates that the actor is under-stimulated and perhaps bored. You might be tired, which is no excuse under these circumstances. Not enough sleep? Nobody gets enough sleep! Including the casting directors.

Perhaps there is not sufficient air intake, which can cause one to yawn. Breathe fully, taking in enough air to fill your lungs, hold for a beat, and then release the air, sighing it out. Repeat this several times before and while you are preparing for the audition. While you are in the midst of the reading, don't wait to take breaths when your lungs have been depleted of air. Take breaths frequently.

If the writer indicates that the character yawns, then go with it. Outside of that, it boggles the mind that an actor would allow an opened-mouth yawn at the reading! At least try to suppress it. You know how. We all know how. I've suppressed many a yawn while watching some auditions!

First Impressions

Your first impression is a lasting one. The audition begins the minute you walk through the door. As one casting director states, "Be somewhat in character." We don't want to see doom and gloom and we don't want to see a hurricane of a person blowing in. Be the best of who you are. Think of your countenance when you walk into a party, filled with attractive, interesting, and accomplished people whom you've not met yet and look forward to meeting. *You* should look like an interesting person as you approach them.

A few casting directors commented on this.

DEBORAH BARYLSKI

I've seen actors talk themselves right out of a job. This covers the actor who feels he has to show us his understanding of the craft of acting by needing every single little detail involving the motivation of the character explained (even if I've already done this and even if it's a one-page scene). It also includes the actor who thinks that the longer he stays in the room, the better his chances are of getting the job. So he starts chattering, trying to be the producer's or director's new best friend. A professional attitude and demeanor are best.

All are in agreement with the following:
If we don't offer our hand to shake with you, don't offer yours to shake with everyone present. It is time-consuming; we have a schedule to keep. Just enter the room or theatre, greet us, do your stuff, and leave. Show us the "best you" that you can. Walk in quietly instead of talking. Do not come on sexually to the casting director. Believe it or not, this has happened more than once. Have a pleasant look on your face as you enter.

Be pleasant and unobtrusive as you are walking in. They're watching you. Don't display a look or posture that connotes tragedy.

GREETING THE AUDITORS

If they don't offer you their hands, don't offer yours. A simple and pleasant hello will suffice. These days, with the knowledge we have regarding the spreading of germs from hand to hand, there are many people who refrain from shaking hands. Don't create a situation where an auditor is forced to acknowledge your outstretched hand with his, and don't put yourself in a position where your gesture is not reciprocated, which will probably leave you feeling abashed, a feeling that certainly will not enhance your performance. Your friendly gesture will most likely be met with annoyance. As the casting directors stated, it is time-consuming and slows down the proceedings. So keep your hands to yourself.

KEEP CONVERSATION MINIMAL

Why would you choose to bother anyone at the audition with a talkathon? The monitor has work to do by checking in you and all the others, calling for the next auditionee and escorting him or her into the audition studio, keeping tabs on who's late and early, giving and receiving forms to be filled out, and periodically talking with the casting director. The actors in the waiting area are (or should be) going over their sides, preparing for their auditions, and trying to stay in character. The auditors in the audition studio have hours of work to do and are trying to see everyone on time within the allotted hours they have access to the studio. Nobody there is interested or has the time to listen to you yapping away. Simply check in, prepare, go into the audition studio or theatre, be polite, take directions, do your audition, and leave.

DON'T LOOK FOR THE CASTING COUCH!

Coming on sexually to the casting director will be met not only with resentment but we will be shocked regarding your abysmal sense of propriety. It will be understood that your ardor is artificial and, chances are, you will be requested to vacate the building immediately.

Unfortunately, I have had male students in my classes who have sexually harassed the female students. When I am told of this conduct and am satisfied that the complaint is a legitimate one, the offender loses his right to continue in the classes.

As a casting director, I have had several males come on sexually to me during pre-audition interviews and in-office auditions. I saw right through them and wanted nothing to do with these individuals; in fact, this was such a turnoff that more often than not an audition was not granted.

There *was* that totally gorgeous one, however, the flirt to end all flirts, who *did* go on to be a major television star . . . No, I didn't fall for it *or* him—and I'll never tell who it was.

YOU AND YOUR EGO

Please come across as a well-adjusted person. Don't display an ego that one could drive a Mac truck through. The casting directors expect you to be pleasant, but don't go overboard.

MICHELLE ALLEN

Obsequiousness interferes with the work. Overt egoism and/or egotism also interferes with the work.

Don't be so busy wanting to be liked and accepted that you perform the scene with this as your underlying motivation. This naturally leads to insecurity—which is what we see.

CATHY WESELUCK

When auditioning for a commercial, don't squander energies by being too concerned whether or not the clients like you personally. Be polite, professional, and be already somewhat in character when you enter the audition room.

The ego is our personal identity, the whole person, self. To be egocentric is to be self-centered, systematically selfish. Those who are extreme egocentrics base their morality on self-interest rather than upon ethics. Egomania is abnormal self-esteem, the habit of talking of oneself, considering only oneself, and behaving in general with way too much self-regard.

All the great actors, the ones whose talents you most admire, suffer from self-doubt each and every time they embark on a production.

All the great actors whose work you admire (for their acting—not beauty or muscle power) have a self-generated interest in and curiosity about human behavior; they are of an inquisitive nature and have concerns about the human plight; they are imbued with a high sense of morality and empathy.

Can you identify yourself as what has just been described?

When a student announces to me that he is going to "own Broadway" or "take Hollywood by storm," I fear that this person is heading for a huge letdown. Of course, you've got to believe and hope that you have something of value to offer as an actor. You must also be open to continue the learning process, and you must want to act with your heart and soul; no other vocation on earth makes any sense to you. But you also know, in your heart, that the struggle to succeed is one tough road, and there is always the possibility that you might not get there. However, you persevere and continue to perfect your craft; you network and audition for small parts in community theatre and Off-Off-Off-Off-Broadway theatre just to be acting and learning and doing what makes you happy and feeling vital and alive.

BROWNNOSING

Do not try to suck up to the casting director or any of the auditors. Give them credit! They *know* when you are trying to ingratiate yourself. Be on time, be pleasant, do your reading, and leave! That is what *they all* say they want! Be professional. You are applying for a job as a professional actor. They don't have to love *you*. They have to love your *performance*.

If you are one who needs to be loved by *everyone* you meet, indulge in some self-analysis. Ask and answer yourself out loud why being loved by everyone and anyone is so essential. If self-analysis doesn't provide answers, go into therapy to rid yourself of a block that will hinder your auditions.

Everyone wants to be liked. We each adhere to social axioms and protocol so as to be accepted as a highly principled, moral, and ethical person and to be liked! If you rely on being liked for who *you* are at the audition, you are neglecting your craft, and you are not servicing your character but only *yourself*. It is you as *character* who is auditioning for the part, not you as yourself. You've got to find that character in you during your preparation, a character perhaps endowed with less than redeeming qualities who is not particularly likeable. Perfectly behaved and highly loved characters don't contribute to dramatic literature as much as those with a cutting edge personality and flaws. With the exception of Mahatma Gandhi, even the great and beloved people who changed the course of history for the better, such as Martin Luther King, Thomas Edison, Franklin D. Roosevelt, and Albert Einstein, had flaws.

ASKING QUESTIONS

You might on occasion have a question or two to ask before the audition. Asking a couple of questions is appropriate. But a barrage of questions is excessive and inappropriate. If more than a couple of questions are asked, the casting directors feel that you haven't done your homework, which means asking and answering the questions *yourself* through the choices you have made for your character's life and the relationship between the characters on the pages.

KELLY MCLAUGHLIN
Don't ask too many questions, thus taking up too much time. Make a choice and do it!

CATHY WESELUCK

It's okay to ask a couple of questions at the beginning of the audition, and many actors don't. Don't feel that you should already know and that asking questions may lessen your credibility or image. Asking questions is important if they are asked in a professional manner and are appropriate.

JUDY HENDERSON

Don't tell us you're not right for the role.

MARSHA CHESLEY

Don't say at a television audition, "I don't watch television."

All agreed with the following:
You should ask a couple of questions if you are unsure of something, but one question you should never ask is, "Is there anything you want to tell me?" You have background information from your agent or on the lead sheet.

Give the casting directors credit for being aware that if there is anything they want to tell you, they will. The casting director or director will give you directions and offer pertinent information after introductions. If you don't understand everything said to you, by all means communicate this. Don't start until everything told to you is clear. The problem is that so many actors are not focused and don't really listen due to their heightened stress. Do some relaxation and breathing exercises in the waiting area to help keep your blood pressure at a close to normal level. Take a couple of deep breaths before you begin the reading.

If they allow you to go right into the reading, that means they have nothing to say to you and are eager to see what you are bringing to them.

I was distressed that one casting director complained that actors don't ask, "do you have any direction for me?" (I won't say who it was.) I asked her why she believed such a question should be asked. Her reply was that sometimes the director changes the concept regarding the character's motivation and interpretation but might not mention this to the actor, or on many occasions he might not be present for the first audition to discuss the changes.

Well, if the casting director has been apprised of the change in concept she has the obligation to communicate the change to the actor without being asked. I cannot conceive of a director or casting director who withholds important information from the actor regarding a major change. The information provided to the actor would most certainly benefit both the actor and auditors. Take my word for it; there may be one director who is guilty of this infraction but the rest will communicate to you any concept changes made regarding your character. I daresay, this director's behavior toward the actor is indicative of inferior directing abilities and might not be a menace any longer; he's hopefully selling shoes somewhere! And shame on the casting director, who should know better than to expect a professional actor to ask such an unprofessional question.

Don't overextend your time by asking a barrage of questions; you must figure things out for yourself and come to your own conclusions. Don't worry if your choices are "right" or "wrong." Get those words out of your vocabulary and thought process. Make choices that you feel good about and go with them.

When you are auditioning for a lead or featured part, you should have made all your inner-life choices, and nobody at the professionally run audition will give you any direction with the exception of where to stand. As professionals, they are aware of the actor's process and would never consider interfering. Well, *many* are aware, that is. I have to admit that some auditors are unaware and insensitive to the actor's preparation process for the audition.

For a commercial audition you probably will be given technical direction: when and how to pick up a prop, what to do with it, where to look if you are not talking to a reader, what facial expressions to make, physical movement wanted, etc.

Tell the Truth, Not the *Whole* Truth

Are you the one who told the casting director at a television audition, "I don't watch television"? ARE YOU CRAZY???!!! Do you believe this is the way to ingratiate yourself with a casting director who makes his or her living through television? Honesty is to be admired. However, honesty should not be the priority in some cases where it can hurt someone, in this case two people. If you don't watch television, just don't mention it under these circumstances. You are not telling a lie. You are just keeping quiet, a virtue!

When one states that he or she doesn't watch television, it is tantamount to saying, "Television is not worthwhile enough to be watched." Arguably, there exists on the tube much substandard programming, but to convey this to a television casting director will not serve you well.

If you don't like television or have only negative feelings about the tube, don't go to television auditions. Chances are, however, that if you inform agents that you won't do television, none will want to represent you. Most of their revenue is derived from television: movies of the week, commercials, doctor dramas, lawyer dramas, police dramas, teacher dramas, sitcoms, miniseries, talk shows, variety shows, news shows, children's shows, comedy specials, musical specials—I think you catch my drift.

5.
ARTISTIC PREPARATION

HERE IT IS, THE BIGGEST COMPLAINT. WHAT DISTURBS CASTing directors more than anything is the actor who is unprepared for the audition. There is work to be done by the actor preceding the audition that, sadly, too many actors are unmindful of.

Unfortunately, many actors don't know how to prepare due to lack of proper acting training. Basic technique and scene study classes are vital to the actor. At least two scene study classes with two different teachers should be taken by every student. These classes train you in communicating, creating, sustaining relationships, and listening. These are all necessary skills for both the rehearsal and the audition process. But some of the guidelines of scene study don't apply to the audition situation. A fine, in-depth acting class with the focus on acting for the audition pulls it all together and provides further insights into how to utilize your acting prowess at the audition.

Most of the casting directors I contacted had strong feelings about the preparedness issue. Here they tell you, in their own words, their analysis of and prescriptives for preparing audition material.

DEBORAH BARYLSKI

Be prepared. This covers not only the preparation as an actor on the scene, but also the business side as well: i.e., not having enough gas or the correct directions ahead of time, so the actor is making a mad dash to the audition, running late, etc. Hence, concentration is not where it should be.

LISA MILLER KATZ

I am constantly amazed at the number of actors who arrive at auditions both without material or any sense of the role that they are reading for. It's important that actors arrive fully prepared, having worked on material that was available to them well in advance of the audition.

LEONARD FINGER

Read the text to determine how your character fits into the action of the piece; many don't.

STEPHANIE GORIN

Obviously the biggest mistake must be not knowing what you are auditioning for. I have seen singers come in for a show like *Rent,* which requires contemporary rock singing, with material from an old time classic musical like *The King and I.* It is so important that you know the show and type of music within the show. I know some actors will be passed over because they have prepared completely the wrong material and seem totally inappropriate for the show. Also it's important that the actor knows his or her age and type. If I'm casting a twenty-year-old, the director doesn't want to see a thirty-five-year-old with good makeup who looks better from a distance.

CATHY WESELUCK

You should adequately prepare your lines, i.e., take enough time to visualize the setting of the scene or approach your reads in different ways (although you are expected to choose one, of course, for the audition itself). Be flexible when the casting director has suggestions. Also, the lines themselves and the intent of them are sometimes not worked adequately, leaving you too tied in to looking down at your script for the sake of security. Though memorization is not required for the audition, actors need to have a certain amount of movement and freedom from the page, which adds to believability.

JANN STEFOFF

Prepare by knowing who the character is, what the character is like, and then make strong choices. It appears that some don't make any choices! Put a twist or slant on the character that is uniquely your own.

SID KOZAK

Don't be ill-prepared. Do your homework and find something new and innovative to a scene. What happens if you don't, is a reading of the text and little attention to the *sub*text.

SANDI NIELSEN

Be prepared. Know the material and do the research thoroughly enough for the audition process. Take an audition seriously. An audition is a job interview. You would go to any other interview dressed appropriately, résumé updated in hand, and with full knowledge of the company and who you are being interviewed by. Show up aware of what you are auditioning for, and with product knowledge.

STUART HOWARD

Be prepared . . . don't try to wing it. Nobody . . . nobody can wing it well.

PATRICIA ROSE

The casting director is the gatekeeper with the responsibility to bring to the director basically those who can play the role. Those capable of pulling it off decide who the character is, what the character is like, then make strong choices. Not making strong choices is the biggest mistake an actor can make. Put a twist or a slant on the character that is uniquely your own.

All agreed on the following:
Take the time to look over a script we have provided. Have knowledge of what you're in for: TV, film, commercial, etc. Ask a lot of questions to your agent; he or she owes you

information about the character and audition. Do your home-work. Be prepared. Know the material and do the research thor-oughly enough for the audition process. Exhibit professional behavior; know the details of the audition. Know who is casting or directing the project. Know why you're at the audition, what you're reading for, what it's about, what the lines are, when the shoot dates are, etc., etc., etc. Give us the impression you're happy to be there, and please, please leave your ego/issues at the door on your way in. Make choices of your own with the material provided. (In other words, don't just read the copy.)

If you have not invested in ample preparation for your read-ing, there is no way you are going to successfully fake it.

WHAT YOUR AGENT SHOULD TELL YOU

Get as much information as you can from your agent about the character and, by all means, know if you are auditioning for theatre, film, or television. When a student of mine has an upcoming audition, I question him or her about details that he or she should be privy to. Too many times, queries such as who is casting the project and questions regarding vital details of the production are met with "I don't know." They don't know because they didn't ask their agents. The agent should com-municate the details without being asked; some don't bother. A well-established mainstream agent who conducts business properly will convey this information to the client. Often the information is on the lead sheet of the audition sides.

You gain insights into the character and the general feel-ing of the audition by being a well-informed actor. You should be well-informed about each and every project. Your agent has the information and should pass it on to you. When the agent gives you instructions as to when your appointment is and where to go, don't stop there. If you have not been given the name of the casting director, the director, and some details regarding the project, just ask. The agent knows but might be in a hurry to get you off the phone for other business. You are entitled to this information; indeed, it is imperative that you are given these details. The more information you have, the more knowledgeable you will be about the script, character, and production, which will give you a feeling of empowerment. You *are* what you *know.*

READ THE SIDES *BEFORE* THE AUDITION

When actors tell me, "They don't give me time to prepare," my reply is, "Don't *allow* them to not give you time; *take* the time!" Empower yourself! Arrive about forty-five minutes to an hour before your scheduled appointment to check in, pick up the sides, and prepare.

Perhaps you already have the sides before you get to the audition. If you are auditioning for a principal (lead role) or minor principal (featured role), your agent should fax or e-mail you the sides a day or two prior to the audition. If you don't have e-mail or a fax or access to a fax at your neighborhood convenience store, your agent can courier them to you, or you might take it upon yourself to simply go and pick them up at your agent's office.

It is my advice that you read the sides—but hold off on making all major choices until you get to the audition. Use the forty-five minutes to an hour to seriously prepare. Allow your performance to be spontaneous. Don't spend hours or days walking around pondering the life and death choices for your character. Your first ones will begin to dissipate after a while and you will probably decide that other and better choices should be made. Beware of this state of mind. You are in danger of falling into an abyss of uncertainty and self-doubt. If you were already cast in the play, you might have the time to try on a repertoire of choices during the rehearsal process. But this is a prep for an audition! You only have one shot! If you don't go with your first, gut feelings, you may begin to search for more interesting ideas, and your choices may become overly intellectualized. The new choices might weaken your commitment to your character and to the relationship between the characters. It just might throw off your entire reading. Avoid this mistake in judgment; if you prepared properly, with full consciousness and awareness, and truly committed yourself to powerful life and death choices, you were right the first time.

The preparation is the key to the audition performance; just like at least four weeks of rehearsals are the key to the opening night performance and two weeks for the camera performance. If there is no preparation, it will be reflected in your reading. Don't blow an audition with an important casting director by not being prepared. If you do, you will go on their you-know-what list!

In a professional audition, when you arrive, the casting director doesn't usually summon you in immediately. You have a time slot for your appointment that was made in advance by your agent.

Choose a peripheral place in the waiting area rather than the center where all the activity is. After removing your outer garments such as your coat, hat, etc., check your mirror to determine that all is well with your hair and face. Then do a relaxation/breathing exercise for a minute or two. If you are not familiar with one, simply close your eyes and slowly take three deep breaths in and out. This will aid in relaxation and bring oxygen to your brain. You will be breathing out the outside world. Push everything from your mind except the sides. Don't make eye contact with the other actors; your eyes are going to be focused on the pages during your preparation. You are not at a social gathering or a meeting place to forge a new relationship.

EMBRACE THE CHARACTER

Get into first person immediately. Don't hold your character at arm's length by referring to him or her in the third person. *Be* the person on the page and be open to feelings that emerge from the dialogue between the two (or more) people. Immerse yourself; he or she will come alive through *your* sensibilities, prejudices, frame of reference, life experiences, desires, fears, and secrets. There is a life on those pages. Don't relinquish yourself; merge with the character.

As this *person* (notice that I am changing "character" to "person" for the preparation), tell yourself that "today is the most important day of my life. Blank [the name of the other person] is the most important person in my life." Then tell yourself, "Today is the most important day of my life because today is the day that I've *got* to change my life, and it has to do with [name of the other person]." "I've *got* to change my life" instead of "I'm *going* to change my life" provides you with more of a sense of desperation and action. (The word is *desperation,* not *desolation.* If you are desperate to achieve an objective, you will fight hard to get it; you will be in an active, engaged, and alive relationship to your wants and needs.) "Got to" is more compelling than "going to." We don't know if we are "going to" succeed at something; we know that we've "got to." If your objective is this urgent, you will start with a strong sense of immediacy, relationship, and positivism—all vital to ensure good communication and a strong stage or screen presence to the auditor, from the very first word of your dialogue.

If you follow through with your character choices in the scene, you will bring a sense of importance and vitality to the reading. Establish an emotional and important relationship with your scene partner (and *you* can do that, even if your reader is the stage manager); it is through the *relationship* that your acting range will be revealed.

You are preparing, not rehearsing. At the audition you will not be reading the entire script, getting off book, being directed, working with the ensemble, making mistakes and correcting them, using props. These are all the properties of a rehearsal, a luxury not available at the audition process.

Now begin reading the sides aloud (not with full projection but yes, aloud) with complete focus, pushing out all other thoughts, images, and life's problems. As you read, if indeed you become unfocused, push your hand out as if you are actually pushing something away and say out loud, "not now, not now, later!" Repeat as needed. This works!

Read the sides including the stage directions. You will not be utilizing them but you might receive some insight into your character. When you have read through the pages, begin to make choices for yourself (as character) starting with the day he or she was born.

MAKING CHOICES

Many of the choices you make for your character's early life leading up to the "here and now" on the pages should come from *your* background. Choose the town where *you* were born if you feel that the character could have been born there. Give your character's father the same occupation as *your* father if you feel it could apply to your character's father; if not, choose another occupation more applicable according to the synopsis and dialogue. What part of town did you live in? How did you get along with your parents? Answer with just a word or two. Don't take up your preparation time on elaborating on the past; just make choices for your character (staying in first person), and move on to the next choice. Did you go to private or public school? How did you get on in school? When you reached puberty and the hormones set in, did you get interested in the opposite sex, or your own? (Yes, are you straight or gay? The sides will, in most cases, indicate your sexual persuasion.) How were your grades in high school? Were you popular? What were your career goals? When and how did you meet the person to whom you are now talking? What happened in your life since high school? What are the important events leading up to this confrontation? (Not "conversation" because I want us to use the strongest terminology possible.) Remember, today is the most important day in your (character's) life!

The reason for creating a history and background is because your character's life didn't begin today (just as yours didn't either). It began eighteen or twenty or thirty years ago with events occurring along the way, culminating in the relationship and circumstance on these pages. By filling in the past from *your* head, *your* world, *your* perception, you are grounding yourself. You will feel more secure, more comfortable, and at one with the character when you step before the casting director.

Finally, ask yourself, as your character, what you desperately need from the other character (use the word "person") that only he or she can give to you that will greatly enhance your life, an emotional need based on love. You desperately need him or her to love you enough and be sensitive to your needs to help you on this day. The dialogue, of course, dictates to you the subject matter and conflicts.

Create your inner life and inner dialogue, what is *not* on the page. This is what some casting directors refer to as "subtext." (Read *Audition* by Michael Shurtleff who, along with this writer, does not like actors to use the word "subtext.")

Prepare by using the *character's* vocabulary, not the *actor's.* Your character would never refer to his or her thoughts as "subtext," just as you and I never do in life situations. Don't editorialize, analyze, or intellectualize; these are words of doom for *any* kind of artist! These words belong in the Fortune 500 arena! This tenet applies also to the rehearsal process when you are developing your character and interpreting the script; make intelligent choices, not intellectual ones. In other words, you should know more than your character does. As the character, don't think, "The reason I am anal retentive is because my mother wasn't demonstrative to me, and I had no father figure for a role model." It's better to have your characters ask themselves questions regarding their feelings and actions, but to not have all the answers. You, the actor, have the answers, but the character does not. The character is in the midst of conflict and searching for answers. Perhaps before the final curtain or scene, he or she might have a breakthrough, but until then, be in each moment. Allow your inner-life choices to fight for a resolution.

WORKING WITH SIDES

No matter how well you connect with your character, or how strong your choices are, your auditors are going to be mightily distracted from your performance if you hold the sides in front of your face or lose your place on the page. Therefore, I am going to tell you the secret to holding the script and sharing your reading so that your wonderful artistic preparation is given the chance to shine.

Hold the sides with both hands allowing your left forefinger or thumb to always be on the line you are reading. You want to take your eyes off the page as much as possible without losing your place. There are three places for you to look: the sides, the person to whom you are talking, and the fourth wall. If the reader is to your side, make sure that you are standing facing downstage (toward the audience). The casting directors want to see your full face, not your profile. They want to see both eyes, not eyelids. So hold the sides up and out, below your chin line.

Keep your right thumb under the lower right hand corner of the page so that you can effortlessly turn each page without breaking your verbal rhythm. Because your hands are on the pages you will not be able to gesticulate. There is no need to do so in a reading but if you must, do it swiftly and get that hand and finger right back where they belong.

EYE CONTACT AND THE FOURTH WALL

The fourth wall is the space in front of you over the auditors' heads. Do not make eye contact with the casting director or any of the auditors during the reading. When you are listening to your reader or the other character(s) in the scene, don't stare at the person; listen and look ahead as you are listening. Look at the other character at pivotal moments, and by all means listen when there are several lines of dialogue spoken to you. Immediately after your line, scan your finger down to your next line and see what the other character's last three words are, memorize them and don't look at the page until you hear those words. In other words, do not read the other character's dialogue; hear it; listen to it.

POSTURE AND MOVEMENT

Stand straight and tall unless it is strongly indicated in the directions that your character is slouching. Put your weight on both feet and do not sway back and forth. Ground yourself. There is no need to move about; for one thing, you don't know how as yet due to lack of character development, which begins during rehearsals *after* you get the part! On camera auditions you must not move around because you have to stay in the camera range.

It is disconcerting to the auditors to watch actors weaving back and forth, standing in a slouch, swinging their arms back and forth, and bobbing their heads. This is almost always unconscious movement that has no relation to the character or the content. All that inappropriate movement makes you difficult to watch; the auditors can't see the character in you.

Be very conscious of your physical movements. Use your body as a prop; it is the best prop you will ever have. Stamp your foot, bend your knees, turn away momentarily, and then turn back; all to make reactions to the conversation taking place between the both of you. But if you find yourself indulging in nervous or repetitive motions with your head, hands, and feet, ask yourself if the character in the situation on the page would be doing these things. At least nine times out of ten, the answer will be a resounding "no."

Take a deep breath, release it, and begin your reading.

ICE-COLD READINGS

In spite of what I have just told you about preparation, some of the finest readings I've seen at casting sessions in New York have been ice-cold. The actors did no preparation whatsoever; in fact, most did not even take a look at the pages in advance of the reading. They were given some minor details regarding the character and situation by their agent or the casting director and then went right into their reading.

However, I have also been witness to disastrous ice-cold readings. My advice to you, if you prefer to read ice-cold, is please take a look at the sides before the read. If you don't, you may succumb to one of the pitfalls that lie in wait for the uninformed: the self-indulgent reading. For example, when doing a comedic piece, you may come across, recognize, and appreciate funny dialogue. Because of its laugh-inducing content, you just might burst out laughing, something the character is *not* supposed to be doing. When this happens it is the actor doing the laughing; this is self-indulgence.

In comedy the audience laughs, not the characters. Comedy is imbued with conflict just as in drama, and the characters are in the midst of turmoil, trying to deal with life's problems. Usually, in comedy, the resolution is a happy one, but until then, the characters are fighting for that happy ending. What is funny to the audience is not funny to the characters.

Audiences love comedy not only because it feels good to laugh (and it's healthy) but also because it serves as a catharsis. The audience will not laugh unless the actor exhibits a keen sense of absurdity and irony—from the inside. It doesn't matter how funny the material is, it is the actor who brings the character to life through his or her humanity. It is the actor who will get the laughs. The audience has to somehow identify with and relate to the situation and the "pain" or "anguish" that the character is going through (yes, in comedy there are these elements). Then they will laugh.

If you read the sides in advance and find "the funny," laugh to your heart's content. Get it out of your system before your reading.

We were doing a scene in class from Neil Simon's *Chapter Two.* George, recently widowed, has just returned to his New York apartment from a European trip made soon after the death of his beloved wife. He is accompanied by his brother Leo, who wants to help George get on with his life. Leo is a fast-talking and fun-loving guy and has a lot of funny dialogue. There is nothing funny about mourning the death of a loved one; however, Leo's dialogue is very funny.

The actor playing Leo had decided to do the scene as an ice-cold reading; he never looked at the sides. All he knew was a very brief synopsis of the scene. As he spoke the lines, he was surprised to see such hilarious dialogue in such a sad scenario, something he never expected.

The actor cracked up with each of the lines. It was he, not the character, who was doing the laughing. His laughter was completely inappropriate. His laughter put a damper on the students in the class who felt cheated; he was doing the laughing for them!

In drama, the content might deal with something terrifying, gruesome, or morbid; it may be something that you as an actor could be personally affected by. Please, for this reason, read the sides in advance so that you are prepared to service your character—not just present yourself. While I teach that you've got to make choices for your character from your head, world, and sensitivities, you've also got to meet the character halfway. In making your acting choices, you must respect the world of the script—to the degree that you have learned about it from the sides—and the character's place within that world. Find that character within you. If you don't, you are being self-indulgent. You must take the

words that the writer has given you and, using your sensibilities, your guts, your frame of reference, give life to those
words. Whomever the writer has conceived of on the page,
that is the character whom you must find within yourself.

There are students who erroneously think the auditors
want to see who the *actor* is during the reading. We are actually looking for a three-dimensional version of the written
character, realized through your flesh and blood. You will
make all the inner-life choices, based upon the script—that
is your job—and you will embody those choices. If you don't
make any choices, or if your choices have little to do with
the material on the page, there is a danger that your performance will come across as empty, vapid, or self-involved.

Preparing for a Commercial Audition

If you are auditioning for a commercial, know what the product is in advance and acquire some knowledge about it. If
you don't use the product, ask someone who is familiar with
it and go to the store that supplies the product. Read the literature on the package.

Are You Right for the Role?

I've always counseled actors to go to any audition where an
appointment can be made even if the actor believes he or
she might not be right for the part. I can tell you honestly
that as a casting director myself, I might be irked when
someone comes before me who physically is the antithesis
of the character in the breakdown, but let him or her give a
superior reading and suddenly the actor becomes the type
we are looking for. We might even consider changing the
type on the pages to fit this actor. It's been done many times.

A few years ago, auditions were being held for a college
production of *Inspector General*, a comedy by the nineteenth-
century Russian writer Nikolai Gogol. All the roles were to
be played by college students, except for the lead role, the

Mayor, which was going to be played by a professional actor who jobbed in. The call in *Back Stage* was for a large, imposing actor who could be funny—a Zero Mostel type. Quite a number of large and imposing actors auditioned, but none quite seemed to satisfy the director. And then, toward the end of the audition day, a small, physically and verbally adept actor showed up—and he got the role! Naturally, many of the director's original concepts for physical comedy were turned on their head by this turn of events. (The Mayor's wife was now much larger than he was!) Granted, this was not, strictly speaking, professional theatre, and it is unlikely that the concept for such a major rolè would change so drastically on Broadway, for example. But stranger things have happened.

Even if the job is ultimately cast according to type, by showing up at the audition and doing a good job, you have given the casting director the opportunity to discover you, perhaps not for the current project but for a future one. When you audition for a specific production, in essence, you are auditioning for future productions also.

This does not mean that you should intentionally approach an audition in a wrongheaded way or audition for something that is outside your skill set. When you are auditioning for a musical and have been given information on what type of material is required, don't deviate and bring something totally inappropriate. Do your research and if the music wanted is not in your range or repertoire, stay away. You are wasting everyone's time and sending the message that says, "I know you don't want the song I am doing, but I don't care and I'm doing it anyway."

6.
BEGINNING YOUR AUDITION

WHEN YOU HAVE COMPLETED YOUR PREPARATION, REMAIN in character, continuing to push outside thoughts away. Your name will be called and you will be escorted into the audition studio or theatre. You will be told where to stand and probably a polite hello will be issued to you with (hopefully) little or no direction. If direction is given, listen very carefully and incorporate at least one direction into your reading. You cannot completely and successfully make major changes on the spot, but do stay alert to one that you might easily be able to incorporate.

The reader (the person reading the other character), a member of the production, might be in a chair or standing a few feet in front of you or perhaps by your side. If the other character is being read by an actor auditioning for the other part, he or she will be standing by your side.

If it is a camera audition, you will do your slate. If not, you will be told by the casting director words to the effect, if not precisely, as I say to actors: "Whenever you are ready."

THE SLATE

When the director and/or clients view the video, the slate is the first thing they will see. This is your introduction to them. The slate procedure will be explained after the casting directors' comments.

LOUISE MACKIEWICZ

Don't deliver an awkward slate to camera, especially a half-hearted profile.

CATHY WESELUCK

Don't hurry into your read immediately after slating. Take a beat or two, or even three to settle yourself in. This little pause in time can make all the difference in focusing on and getting into the character.

Don't ask questions as the slate is about to begin. Ask them up front before we announce we will now begin with the slate.

The camera audition begins when the casting director tells you to do your slate. This means that when you audition for film or television, you will be asked to look into the camera, state your name and the name of your agent. You might be asked to turn to the right and then to the left. Immediately after doing this you begin your reading.

You are always taped when auditioning for a film or for television. Once the film is rolling, the audition has begun and your slate is the first part of the audition. If you ask a question after your slate, the tape will have to be erased. This is a great annoyance to the auditor running the camera. I know firsthand. I was guilty of this infraction once. Ask your questions before the slate.

You should have been somewhat in character when you entered the studio, but also attuned to your surroundings and to those conducting the audition. When you slate, allow yourself, as actor, to be the one slating, not the character.

Do your slate in a professional manner. Look into the camera and announce your name and the name of your agent loudly and clearly. When asked to turn to the left and then to the right, turn all the way to enable the camera to film you totally in profile. Convey your professionalism by showing that you actually enjoy doing your slate. It is an important part of your audition.

Auditors are instantly displeased with an auditionee who presents the slate in a lackluster manner. I've been witness, as have many casting directors, to halfhearted presentations, and we wonder why the actor even showed up. If the actor appears bored or uninterested, we lose interest. (If we lose interest as early as the slate, we will probably fast-forward the tape past the audition when we are reviewing it.) By and large, when a slate is badly delivered, it is followed by an inferior reading. The well-prepared actor excels in both presentations.

After the slate, give yourself a few seconds to settle yourself, as casting directors suggest. If you spent your time preparing in a productive manner, it should not take you long to make the transition back into character. I dislike the word transition, but in this instance you need to be able to make that switch from you the actor to you the character. One way to help yourself through this transformation, so that you don't feel like you are starting out cold, is to slightly shift your point of focus. Allow yourself as character to see something on the back wall. Make one simple change to your physicality (inhale, shift your weight, etc.), that assists in grounding you in the scene. It really helps to give yourself a clean starting place.

7.
TAKING DIRECTION

ONE DAY I WAS WAITING TO AUDITION WHEN THE CASTING director caught sight of me. She hurriedly told me that my character would not be wearing the kind of jewelry I had on and strongly suggested that I go to the ladies room and remove all of it and also remove some of my makeup. "Quick," she added, "before the director sees you." I had a friend at this audition. No, not an old friend. I had never seen her or auditioned for her before.

The casting director is there to assist you in many ways. She (or he) is not your enemy.

CRAIG ALEXANDER
When we give directions please listen.

MICHELLE ALLEN
Don't be so committed to choices (rigid) that you are unable to take direction. Listen to directions. Some actors marry themselves to an idea and won't shake it no matter what advice the casting director gives them.

CHRISTY L. POKARNEY
When given direction by either the casting director or director don't continue on with the audition in your own manner.

JULI-ANN KAY

Do not look at the auditors in a questioning way but have an open mind toward our instructions. When a direction is given, do not say, "I don't feel comfortable with that." We may just say, "Run with it," but we may also give important advice.

All agreed on the following:
Please do not argue with the casting director over anything! Trust the casting director. We really know what we are doing.

Clear your head, be focused, and listen. Some actors' high level of tension at the audition renders them incapable of the proper focus and concentration to listen and absorb what is being said to them. If you have been trained as an actor, you know how important it is to be able to really hear and react to your scene partner—employ those listening skills when the casting director makes suggestions! If the director or casting director issues direction that is beyond an actor's capability, it is immediately apparent. The reading will be stopped and the actor will be thanked and sent on his way.

LISTEN TO YOUR DIRECTOR

When the casting director talks, listen, believe, and trust! Hopefully you prepared for your character with self-assurance regarding your choices, but if the casting director offers you information contrary to your view, be smart. Be open to the direction and incorporate it into your reading. With sufficient and proper training, you will have the ability to include these new insights given to you.

The casting director has read the script several times and has had meetings and discussions with the director. Casting directors serve their directors so when the casting director tells you anything, more likely than not, it is actually coming from the director.

PHYSICAL DIRECTION FOR MOS/SOC AUDITIONS

You get heavy-duty direction when you audition for a commercial with no dialogue or a scene with no dialogue. In the waiting room when you check in, you will be given a piece of paper containing cartoon drawings of each frame as the action progresses (storyboards). Study it carefully. When you enter the audition room, the casting director will direct you as to the attitude of the character, facial expressions, physicality, and overall demeanor. Listen, absorb, and follow these directions.

COMBINING YOUR CHOICES WITH THE DIRECTOR'S

When there is dialogue involved and you have already made your choices in the waiting area, the casting director might give you direction such as, "Your character has a dislike for and is suspicious of the other character."

Perhaps you have already made a choice that your character is crazy about the other character because there is nothing on the pages to suggest that you are not crazy for her or him and because it is a good choice to make as your mystery and secret. But the casting director knows what has transpired before and after the scene where it is perhaps revealed why you would not be so crazy about the other character. Take the direction and without discarding your own choices, add the element of suspicion by conjuring up fear that you (your character) might be misled by the other character's words and/or actions and that it is imperative that he or she proves your suspicions are unwarranted.

Saying, "I don't feel comfortable with that" is tantamount to saying, "I don't want to audition for you so I'll just be on my way."

If the directions given to you regarding the interpretation are at variance with yours, be diplomatic and don't dispute the difference. Try to include something of the direction to your already prepared version.

Quite a long time ago, I was auditioning for a movie of the week. I had made all my inner choices, including the choice that I (my character) did not know that the other character in the scene had murdered several people, and that my life might be in danger. I was attracted to him and thought he had a cutting edge personality, which I found exciting. There was no indication in the scene of the male character's nefarious deeds. I, Ginger, had read the character breakdown, so I knew that he was a murderer, but my *character* didn't know this.

Right before the slate, the director talked to me and told me that I should play the audition as if I knew about my scene partner's crimes, and as if I was afraid of him. In fact, according to the script, the murders were not revealed to my character until the end of the movie, after the scene in question. I knew enough not to debate the issue with the director (actually I was shy and intimidated by him), so I added as my mystery and secret that I suspected he might be the murderer but hoped he wasn't because I liked him so much.

My reactions to some of his dialogue changed due to this suspicion, and, I must say, it enhanced my performance because it added anxiety and doubt. I didn't *know* he was the murderer, as the director instructed me; I chose to be suspicious and worried that he might be the murderer and that my life might be in danger. I took the direction given, but bent it slightly to accommodate my integrity. It worked. I got the part.

However, if the problem you have is not one of interpretation but with the script itself, this may not be the job for you. If the dialogue offends you in some way then obviously you should not be auditioning for the production. Scripts are written to express the way people talk. Perhaps it's not the way you talk; you have every right to leave.

Many casting directors will give you no direction, in which case they are open to whatever you will be doing for them. They assume that you have gone over the sides and have done your part as actor by making choices for your character and that you require no further information from them. At times, it is the director who has instructed the casting director to withhold direction. He wants to see what you are bringing to him on your own.

Whether or not you are given direction, it is in your own interest to prepare professionally with choices for and attitudes as the character, situation, and conflict on the pages. This preparation will allow you to go with the flow in character. If you have not made your choices, then you will have to make them spontaneously as you read the sides and improvise your way through the audition. While I've mentioned previously that some of the best auditions I've ever seen have been ice-cold, in most cases the actors who performed them were well-trained and very experienced, and knew how to make choices on their feet. They had learned the rules and therefore knew how and when to break them. I must note that there really is no single set of hard and fast *rules* for actors. Different actors succeed using different approaches, but all actors need *guidelines.*

Finally, if you don't want the part, by all means argue with the casting director. This will assure you of being out on the street within a minute.

No Second-Guessing

Don't try to get into the casting director's or director's head. You'll drive yourself crazy. If you try to make yourself into what you guess they want, you will cripple yourself and end up not showing them the best of your work. Directors have been known to say after a reading about the actor, "I don't know where he or she got it. I don't know how he or she got it. I just love it."

Well, you didn't get it from them or anyone except from *your* head, *your* perceptions, *your* world, *your* frame of reference, *your* guts—with a little help from the writer. See what the casting directors have to say about this.

STUART HOWARD

Don't try to guess what the casting director/director/producer is looking for. Some of the time, we don't know ourselves, but if we see an actor presenting himself or herself to the best of his or her ability and it strikes a chord, there will probably be a callback.

SANDI NIELSEN

Don't try too hard to stand out. Unfortunately many actors spend a lot of time trying to be unique, but not necessarily in a positive way. Talent is the ultimate power.

All were in agreement with the following:
Don't try to second-guess us. Sometimes we have no idea what we're looking for, but when "the one" walks in, we know it immediately. Don't give us what you think we want when we don't even know ourselves. You should present what you want to give and have the courage to take the risk by not worrying if that is what we are looking for.

You give what you think we want, but often it's the one who gave something else who gets the callback because that actor gave something we never thought of and we loved it. Never comment on your performance. We may have loved what you did. Give 100 percent and then move on.

You should not involve yourself in wasted energy by trying to give them what you think they might want. They have a general idea of what they are looking for, but they are open and waiting for something better that you can bring to them. What excites casting directors is discovering a performance that brings a whole new dimension to the character.

Here's a story wherein the casting directors knew just what they were looking for—until they found something better. New York actor Joseph Small was once called to audition for a commercial for America's Best Contacts & Eyeglasses.

The commercials were supposed to feature a Ross Perot look- and sound-alike. The actor was called because he met the height and weight requirements for the role, although in reality he sounds and looks almost nothing like Perot. But, being a diligent and professional actor, he says, "I actually worked up quite a good Ross Perot. But I went to the initial auditions and I kept hearing the guys before me doing Ross Perot (some better than me), and I thought it sounded bor- ing. I went in and did a southern preacher character (I'd done the character in a *Spoon River Anthology* production years earlier). I got called back. At the callback it came down to me and a dead-ringer for Ross Perot. I got the job and ended up doing five commercials. Finally I asked the direc- tor why they chose me, and he said 'there was joy in your reading, and there was no joy in Ross Perot.'"

You've got to show that you are hooking up to what the writer has given to you regarding the character, the relation- ships, and the situation on the page, but it is the actor who adds another level to the character who will get the callback.

Give them what *feels good to you!* Don't concern yourself with whether it's right or wrong. Eliminate those two words from your vocabulary. Go with your feelings, which are based on the inner-life choices you have made.

Don't Try to Be Unique

I love what Sandi Nielsen said: "Talent is the ultimate power." Beautiful and true!

Your talent will get you the part. Don't try to get the casting director to remember you by exhibiting behavior reflecting anything other than the character's individuality. Don't try to be unique. That effort has no relation to acting. Perhaps your character is construed by you to be unique, whatever that means. Your character is human; therefore, you already share many qualities. Everyone is unique in his or her own way. Don't do something inorganic to try to stand out. Previous and sufficient acting classes taken by you should have prepared you to resist trying to be unique. Show the casting director that you have an understanding of the character and that you are deeply immersed in the relationship between the characters. Do your preparation, be pleasant to others, and do your reading. If your performance is "right on," you will be unique because you will be one of the few who will be granted a callback.

WE WANT YOU TO SUCCEED!

If the casting director has granted you the audition, then he or she thinks that you might be right for the role. The casting director is in a better position to make these decisions than you are. One casting director beautifully states it as follows:

LIZ RAMOS
Remember why you are there. You are all winners. There is a reason why you are there. It's like being nominated.

Why on earth would you want to put a bug in the casting director's ear indicating that you're not comfortable with the part, that you don't think you are right for it? Casting directors expect that you will identify with the character, accept the challenge, and most certainly that you will *want* to play the character. So much of the job of being an actor is getting the job, so try to see the fact that the casting director called you in as a vote of confidence in your talent and professionalism. You are a winner, and you are right for the job, or they wouldn't have wasted their time.

Of course, if you don't want the part, do say that you feel you are not right for it and the part will most definitely go to someone else.

Perhaps you don't identify with the character. Could it be that you are not allowing yourself to identify with the character because you are nervous or afraid? Think about it. You have more in common than you realize. If you do your work properly, if you focus and concentrate, you will find similarities in *something* on the sides or in the inner life of the character, choices that come from you, not the writer.

The writer writes only half a play or film. You, the actor, must write the other half, the actor's half.

Prepare, making strong life-and-death choices for your character based on *your* life, *your* head, *your* perceptions, *your* soul, *your* guts, *your* frame of reference, *your* fantasies, *your* desires. Find that character within you, and go for it. Don't be afraid of being too big. Be honest in every way in your preparation; with total honesty there is no such thing as being too big.

8.

USING THE SPACE

IT IS NOT APPROPRIATE TO DIRECT YOUR AUDITION. CREATE, don't direct. Approach your audition from *inside* the character; do not preplan intricate blocking or other effects that will prevent you from being in the moment. Directing is external and is the job of the director. At the audition you simply stay put, using your body as a prop, and perform. There are no hand props and there should be a minimal amount of physicality on your part.

KELLY MCLAUGHLIN
Don't use props in the audition. (Fake babies are distracting.)

MARSHA CHESLEY
Don't make an audition into an exercise in blocking or pantomime. Don't stage the scene. Just find the emotion in the scene and deliver the lines.

CATHY WESELUCK
Actors often do not use their space as much as they could in the audition. Although you are limited to a specific area due to camera restrictions, etc., you could, where appropriate, widen your scope of contact visually and with your body when you are reading. Again, this adds to believability.

As I tell my students, your body is the best prop you will ever have. At the audition there is no need for props of any kind. It is a reading, not a rehearsal. Even in the very early stages of rehearsals, no props are used.

STRONG, SIMPLE MOVEMENTS

At the audition, a prop is an intrusion. You will be believed if you mime an action and keep it to a minimum. Allow your body to express passion by swift strong movements (in place) while still holding the sides and not losing your place. Mime the glass your character is holding for a moment and then let it go. I don't recommend that you mime the phone your character is holding because your left hand's index finger should always be pointing to the line being spoken (to enable you to take your eyes off the page as much as possible) and your right hand should be holding the pages on the bottom right-hand corner under the page you are reading (to enable you to turn the page without wasting time and interrupting your verbal rhythm). However, there are moments when you can remove your hand from the sides to gesture or mime. Return your hand to the paper immediately following the physicality.

THE CASTING DIRECTOR'S SPACE

The audience does not want to be in your scene. The casting director is your first audience. He has his space and you have yours. Make sure there is space between the two.

PATRICIA ROSE
Don't invade the casting director's space.

All the casting directors were in agreement on the following:
I don't want your physical presence right on top of me. I can't evaluate your performance properly. I don't want to be in the

audition. I want to be a spectator. Don't keep getting closer
and closer as you do the reading.

If you are auditioning on camera you will, of course, have a
designated place to stand. When there is no camera your
audition place is also designated, usually several feet from
the auditor. Your space should be confined to an imaginary
line surrounding you no more than two feet in diameter.

In Los Angeles and Toronto casting directors will often
read with you, instead of using a reader. The director will
sit on a chair, several feet before you, near the rest of the
auditors. You certainly do not want to invade the casting
director's space. It makes the casting director very uncomfortable to have you bearing down on him or her. You
want to make it seem as if you might be about to approach,
but don't.

In fact, no matter who your reader is, communicate
strongly but keep your distance. This is partially a practical
matter; if you move in very close to the reader while holding
the sides in your hand, there is a chance that you may trap
or upstage yourself. Then the auditors won't be able to see
you properly. Of course, if you are doing an on-camera audition you must stay put, or you will not be in the frame. For
theatrical auditions you have more freedom to move, but do
remember that a lot of gesticulation and pacing will only dissipate the power of your performance or obscure the auditor's view of you.

The auditors are the audience and you are the per-
former. They do not want to be your scene partner. I teach
that your audience is a participant in your performance,
not due to physical proximity but because your powerful
inner-life choices, imbued with emotional outreach, demand
the audience's engagement. And the audience wants to

identify (empathize) with you, relate to you, sympathize with you, cry over you, laugh at your humor, fall in love with you, hate you—in other words, be affected by you. At the audition, the casting director wants to be affected in that same way. If the audience believes you, you have won them over. If the casting director believes you, chances are you will get a callback.

Hopefully you took a good How to Audition class, and by that I mean one that is an in-depth acting class, not one that boasts, "This is not an acting class!" A class that gives you a purely technical approach to the audition doesn't teach you about *acting* for the audition. It covers facial movements, where to stand, how to slate, and how to feel comfortable with the camera. It appears that some individuals are camera shy and uneasy in front of one. Too bad, because as actor, you have nothing to do with the camera! Unless you are a spokesperson or except when you are doing your slate, you don't look at the camera and must never think of the camera as being anywhere near you.

When you get the part the director explains the physicality and the blocking of the scene to you before the shoot. Scenes can and usually will be reshot several times. Although the process of making a movie is quite different than the process of producing a play, there is no difference between camera acting and theatre acting—except vocal projection. (If you have ever been fortunate enough to see Al Pacino perform on stage, you will have noted that his acting and body language are no different in the theatre than they are on film.) You must convey the same amount of emotional intensity and passion. In a theatre audition you don't move about, either, because you haven't learned how yet. Physicality emerges with character development, none of which exists at the reading audition.

So, whether you are auditioning for the stage or the screen, you want to keep movement to a minimum. Respect the space of your auditors and of your scene partner, and make sure that your body is alive and ready to move even when you are very still. Use your body as a strong, simple, expressive prop.

9.
PERFORMING THE AUDITION

YOU'VE GLEANED AS MUCH INFORMATION ABOUT THE CHARacter as you could from the words you were given, and you're holding the sides correctly, so that you can see the page while allowing the auditioners to see your face. You are ready to read. But just how sacred are those words? Can you ad-lib if it helps you or if you think you've found a better way to state the writer's intent?

You are not the writer; at least not at the audition. Your obligation is to read exactly what is on the pages. There are liberties to be taken, however.

CLARE WALKER

Try to stick with the lines that are written rather than change them around in the audition to suit yourself. You never know when the director has written it. Or if you really must, ask permission to change the lines.

The casting directors were in agreement with the following: Don't indiscriminately and blatantly change dialogue. Don't invert words, substitute words, or leave out words. This doesn't make sense, as the writer or writers will be offended.

Speaking the dialogue as written certainly applies to auditioning for theatre. For the new play there is a playwright out there who has been at his paper and quill (or at least a typewriter; so many writers refuse to use computers) for the past year or two, then patiently suffered while his or her agent submitted the play to producers, the sixth of whom finally optioned the play. The playwright is now watching and listening to you read lines from his "baby." It's an interesting dichotomy that the playwright's goal is to get his play produced, yet during preproduction, despite being thrilled to be working toward an opening night, he also begrudges the casting director, director, set designer, lighting designer, stage manager, and, yes, even the actors taking a piece of his "baby." It's tantamount to suffering through a lengthy labor and finally giving birth—only to have others raise the child. He is in the third row of a darkened theatre near the casting director and director or sitting with them behind a table ten feet away, staring at you in an unadorned, neon-lit, windowless, unclean, referred-to-euphemistically-as-a "studio," in a sick building utilized for casting sessions, rehearsals, and acting workshops, with the scent of stale cigarette butts wafting through the air. (Ah, yes, the glamour of show business.)

If you dare to change a *single word*, he might become apoplectic. Playwrights will say, "If I wanted it written that way, I would have written it that way."

I have, on the other hand, heard playwrights express interest in hearing actors deviate from the words on the page. These are usually neophyte writers or those who have exhausted their limited writing ability and are desperate for help from *anyone*—including the washroom attendant—and the production is usually a second-class one. If you dislike the dialogue because it feels stilted to you or unnatural or silly, do your part as actor and bring what's on that page to life through your intelligently made acting choices. Give your opinions to your character!

Allow your character to also be aware that what you are saying is stilted, unnatural, or silly. We do that in life. Sometimes we admit that how we expressed ourselves was really stupid. Why not the character? You say, well, maybe the character really isn't aware of his stupid remarks. Yes, this might be the case. So don't be aware, but also allow the opposite side of you to feel that what you are saying might just be stupid. (For a lengthier explanation of this technique, read *Audition* by Michael Shurtleff.)

When you get the part, have signed the contract, and rehearsals are under way, then you may diplomatically discuss the offending or awkward lines with the director. When you become a star and are therefore "bankable," you have the prerogative to register any complaints you may have regarding the dialogue upon reading the script. The writer will often accommodate the star.

REWRITING THE DIALOGUE

Often the playwright is amenable to listening to your input and indeed making the changes you request—during the rehearsal process, *not* during the audition. But please, adhere to protocol. First discuss your desire to make changes with the director, *not* the playwright. Contractually the playwright has the final word but it is the director who works directly with the actors, not the playwright. By and large when the playwright has notes for the actors, he discusses them with the director who then passes them on to the actors; therefore, the same chain of communication should be respected when the suggestions are going in the opposite direction.

At the audition, due to nervousness, actors leave out or add a word or two or invert a line. This infraction can be tolerated if done once during a reading. We probably won't see it as a case of blatant editing, but if it's done more than once, watch out. Then it appears that we have a rewriter on our hands and the real writer and/or director will be offended.

Obviously, when auditioning for a revival, one does not change a word. It is tried-and-true dramatic literature and has earned the right to prevail as is—that is, unless the director has taken liberties with the script, which is permissible only by consent from the playwright. If the play is in the public domain the director may do whatever he wishes with the script.

When auditioning for a film or television script, you might be told when given the sides that if you wish, you may improvise, rewrite, or substitute words at your discretion. This means, more often than not, that the writer and director (often the same) are not satisfied with what is currently on those pages and they are open to what you, the actor, might be able to contribute. Often the script is written by a committee of writers and what ends up on the pages is a mishmash of their words and lines of dialogue. It's not as if there is one writer whose work is his "baby" and whose fragile self-esteem is on the line. Or the auditioners may want to see if your spirit is free enough to improvise. For the beginning actor, these suggestions might be intimidating. You have studied acting, not writing. You have enough work to do concentrating on your preparation. It is not your job to have to come up with new dialogue. Go with the flow. If something should happen to crop up during your preparation or even during the reading, do it. Otherwise, just do what you were trained to do. Make your acting choices and stick to the dialogue.

If you do change any dialogue, make sure the cues remain the same. Assuming it is a two or more character scene, the reader or actors reading the other parts must be given the original cues.

One casting director suggested that if you really must, ask permission to change the lines. I believe that you should not "really must." However, if a word is considered by you to be an obscenity that puts you into an extremely uncomfortable mode and the uttering of it would compromise your principles and integrity, you might ask permission to change it. Your objection to the word might cost you the part if the writer or director will not accept a substitute word. On the other hand, if your performance is outstanding, your value to the production is escalated and that word diminishes in value. The word will be banished. You will prevail.

Once I was told to rewrite the entire audition if I wanted to. I took the page home, looked at it, and thought, "This is supposed to be humor but I don't think it is very funny."

So I rewrote the entire page. It was dialogue for just my character talking to the other one. I wrote what I considered to be much funnier material than what was on that page. I did the audition; they all laughed like hell. I got a callback and got the part.

STARTING OVER

You start the reading, but you just feel you are on the wrong track. It is tempting to want to stop and start again. Under certain circumstances, this can be done.

SHASTA LUTZ

Know the scripts. We'll help you with the delivery. Remember there is a general assumption that on the day of the shoot a good actor will have remembered the lines. If you screw up in the middle of a read, just throw in some words. It's the delivery and expressions and voice I'm concerned about. Don't keep asking to start again. Once up front is enough.

All the casting directors agreed on the following:
If you must start again let it be within the first line or two, no later. When we know immediately that we don't like what we are seeing, we will either stop the reading completely or sometimes give you suggestions on how to improve it and allow you to begin again, but only if we see some qualities that we find appealing. Instead of starting over you should change the delivery at the moment you realize the reading is not going well. Save yourself.

Almost all casting directors resent being asked by the auditionee if he or she may start again if the reading has already progressed beyond the fourth or fifth line. Either they will begrudgingly say yes or they might have seen enough to actually like the reading or are only too ready and willing to dismiss the actor because of a poor reading. Be careful; when you ask to start again you are presenting them with the opportunity to end the audition. Often, after just one line of dialogue, the casting director knows if you are right for the part!

If you feel you started off on the wrong foot, simply get on the right foot! Change in midstream. If you are well prepared and had a strong and positive moment before, and are focused, there will be no need to start again.

If you are stopped and given direction by the casting director, listen, absorb, and respond to the suggestion. The casting director is helping you by giving you another chance.

Some casting directors feel you should start over if the reading has gotten off on the wrong foot. If you are just a couple of lines into the reading, there's no damage done. You probably are safe and will be allowed to start again. But I still believe the best way is to change in midstream. Psychologically, it's better for you, because you will refocus without disrupting your own performance.

BEING OFF BOOK

Most of the time you will not be required to be off book at the audition (that is, to have memorized the lines). But at times you will be asked to learn the dialogue.

CLAIRE WALKER

Be off book when asked to be. Once you glance down at the page you are out of character.

Marsha Chesley

Memorize the sides but then hold on to the pages just in case. The actor gets flustered if he forgets a line and doesn't have the pages in front of him.

Most of the casting directors don't want you to be off book and concurred with the following:
If you make the decision to be off book and then realize that you don't know the lines as you thought you did, you will get flustered and might have to improvise. We don't appreciate this.

By and large, you will not be expected to be off book at an audition. If, however, like Ms. Walker, the casting director feels that looking down at the page breaks the character's continuity, she may ask you to memorize the lines. If you are instructed to do so, comply. Why would an actor not follow directions from the casting director? Should it not be clear to the actor that by ignoring the request, he or she is demonstrating disrespect and a lack of professionalism?

If you are auditioning for a lead or featured part and have had the sides for two days or less, you probably won't be expected to be off book. However, if you are auditioning for an under five (five lines or less; in the United States, this is called a day player; in Canada, it is called an actor's part), there should be no reason why you shouldn't learn those very few lines quickly and require no sides in your hands. Don't forget to memorize your cues!

Also, don't take it upon yourself to memorize a sizable amount of dialogue and then take the risk that you might go up on a line or freeze. Here's a psychological truth: If you audition without the book in your hand, you are inviting the casting director to judge a finished performance. If you retain the script, you remind the viewers (and yourself) that you've only had the material for a short time. If you weren't instructed to memorize, don't.

Losing Your Place

Losing your place on the page and losing your focus because you don't know where you are can certainly cause you to fail at your audition.

> *All the casting directors were in agreement:*
> Be careful not to lose your place. Pay attention to your sides, or else you will have to fumble to find your place. If this happens repeatedly we feel we have to stop the reading.

As I mentioned earlier, I teach my students to hold the sides with both hands with the right thumb under the lower right-hand corner page. As each page is turned, the right thumb should immediately go under the next page. This facilitates a swift turning of each page. The left index finger or thumb should be pointed toward the lines as spoken and should continually be moving down the page. This will prevent you from losing your place.

In life we lose our place. We often forget what we are saying. It takes a few beats to get back on track. In the audition, if you lose your place, lose it in character: Don't panic; find it and continue. Allow your character to have "lost it."

However, if you are holding the sides correctly, why are you losing your place? You are not properly focused on the here and now, meaning exactly what is going on between the characters. You haven't committed yourself thoroughly to the relationship and events on the pages. Perhaps you were one of the actors who didn't work on the sides while you were in the waiting area, bringing outside events with you. You decide why you lose it and then don't do it anymore.

Where to Look

Actors have a problem of where they should be making eye contact. It's not so difficult.

All the casting directors are in agreement with the following: Don't bury your face in the pages. Don't stand in profile so auditors or camera can't see your full face. Several times during the reading, look at the reader. This is the other character to whom you should be looking. Don't look down at the floor. We want to see your face and your eyes.

There are three places you should be looking during the reading: the page (as little as possible), the reader or actor auditioning for the other part in the scene, and the fourth wall (everything you see in front of you above the auditors' heads).

One of the worst mistakes you can make at the audition is to bury your head in the sides. When my students do this, I tell them that it appears that they are having a relationship with the pages, not the other person. And, indeed, that's how it will look to the casting director who will hardly be able to see your face, let alone see how you are relating to the other character!

You must get your eyes off those pages and make contact with the other character. When you are listening to someone as she talks, what do you look at on her face? The eyes. Why do so many actors deprive the auditors from seeing eyes? We want to see eyes, not eyelids. We want to see two eyes, not one. Don't stand in profile. I have heard that there are a few acting teachers who have advised actors to stand in profile. Don't listen to them! They are dead wrong!

At some auditions you will be reading with the casting director or a designated reader representing the production. For a camera audition, this person usually sits a few feet in front of you, facing you, near the camera, which will have a full view of your face as you perform with the reader. Do not look at the camera. The reader is the other character and it is to him or her that you will be talking and looking. At other auditions (theatre or camera), you will be reading with an actor reading for the other part in the scene who will stand beside you. It is this physical setup that causes actors to play in profile.

Stand facing downstage (toward the audience or camera) and turn your head, using your neck, not your body, to look at the other character at pivotal moments in the script. You need not stare at him or her constantly.

On the other hand, why would you not occasionally look at the person to whom you are talking and listening? We do it in life. Why not at the audition? You must make eye contact several times during the reading. You must express yourself with your voice, emotions, facial muscles, and eyes.

In life when we are distressed, saddened, depressed, etc., we have a tendency to look down. As I've stated before, the truth of life does not always transfer well to the truth of acting. When an actor looks down during the audition, he or she is alienating the other character and therefore the audience. When your character is immersed in a negative mode, don't look down. Look out at the fourth wall. Expose and share your feelings. It will seem to the audience (at the audition, the casting director) as if you are looking down.

Never look at the floor or the ceiling. You are out there for just a few minutes. Don't waste your valuable time alienating us as you look at the floor. Don't allow the camera or the auditors to see so much of the white of your eyes when you look up. It's very unflattering.

VIOLENCE IN AUDITION SCENES

There should be no physical acts of violence in the audition. Don't deliver any blows to your fellow actor.

All the casting directors were in agreement with the following: Do not be physical with violence within the scene at the audition even if the script calls for it. Mime as much as you can. With violence, we get frightened and almost forget everything else. If you get physical, we stop the reading. That doesn't belong at the audition. We are wary of the actor who resorts to harsh physicality at the audition. Even if it is in the script, we don't want it yet.

There is no place for this kind of behavior at the audition. A young man lost his hearing when, during a reading, the other actor walloped him on his face and head. The stage direction called for this action but it must not be executed without the direction of a combat choreographer.

A real slap, kick, punch, or other violent action should never be executed during an audition. Without rehearsal, and with the extra added energy and anxiety that the audition situation can foment, it is just too easy to miscalculate the action and hurt or frighten your reader or the auditioners, neither of which will help you to get the part. If a stage direction tells you to physically assault the other character, you should slap the air in front of the reader's face. Before you begin your reading, tell the person of your plan to do this. If you are the one to be assaulted, ask the actor before you begin to kindly not slap you.

If the reader is sitting several feet in front of you, in which case the reader is probably the casting director, slap the air in front of you as if you are slapping him. Do not approach the casting director and frighten him.

After you are hired, you will learn during the rehearsal process how to execute the violence without damaging anyone.

10.

THE MONOLOGUE AUDITION

ONOLOGUES ARE CALLED FOR AT THEATRE AUDITIONS AND
when auditioning for an agent. You should have at
least two monologues completely prepared, although four
would serve you even better. Theatre casting directors sit
through about ten to twenty monologue auditions within an
hour, depending on whether the audition calls for one or two
pieces to be performed. Can you imagine how disheartening
it must be for them to be subjected to a day of inactive, passive, stagnant, and inappropriate material? The reality is that
too many monologues done at auditions are poorly chosen
and do not display the strengths of the actor. Is it any wonder that such material does not inspire callbacks?

All the casting directors agreed with the following:
Be at ease during your monologue auditions. Be comfortable
with your body language. Make sure to bring monologues
that are right for what we are casting. You should have been
given a character breakdown in advance; take it seriously and
choose a monologue from your repertoire that feels appropriate for the play you are auditioning for. Bring a comedic piece
when you are auditioning for a comedy and vice versa. This
makes sense.

Speak up and project when you are auditioning for a theatre piece. You must know that we require a strong voice.

We sometimes ask for two contrasting monologues and many actors say they only have one, or if they have two, they're very similar. We don't get to see the actor's range.

If you go blank in the middle don't just stand there. You should just go on and say whatever pops into your head regarding the character.

When you have been instructed to bring in a monologue not longer than two minutes make sure it is not three or four minutes. We don't like to stop you but if we do, please don't get angry with us. We have allotted two minutes to all actors and we want to make sure we see them all. Actually, a minute and a half is just fine with us. If you've chosen the right material, we can easily evaluate your acting within that time.

Don't lock eyes with me forcing me to feel that I am in the scene. I am not the other character.

A monologue is a two-character scene. For two minutes you happen to be doing all the talking; the other character is doing the listening. The worst way to look for a monologue is to look for a monologue! The dialogue should deal with the here and now and the person (character) to whom you are talking. When you choose a piece written as a monologue, it is, by and large, a memory piece, meaning the action is past-tense and, therefore, passive. The character is talking about events that have happened in the past, just telling a story. The casting director does not want storytelling. With this kind of material, the actor cannot create a relationship between the two characters. There is no emotional reachout or emotional action; the actor is simply talking about a past event, which is uninteresting in a monologue audition. It is through the relationship that the casting director can see the actor's range.

Stop pouring through those monologue books in search of the perfect monologue; it's not there. That is why I wrote the book, *The Perfect Monologue,* telling actors why they should not buy monologue books! See and read *plays!* At least once each and every week! Create your own monologues from already existing published and produced plays. Note that I said *create;* I didn't say write them. Let the writer do that.

CHOOSING MATERIAL WISELY

Think of all the plays you have seen or read throughout your adult life. There must be one or more that affected you strongly in some way, any way; it doesn't matter as long as you had a strong emotional reaction to it. There is a hidden monologue in that play for you. Don't concern yourself with the age range, gender, or race of the character whose dialogue you identify with and relate to. As long as it's not in the *dialogue* that the character is of an age nowhere in your range or that the character is of a different race or gender, there is no reason why you can't do the material and make it your own.

Get the play and read the scene(s) that you relate to. Read *only* the dialogue of the character to whom you relate. What will happen eventually (if not immediately) is that a line of your dialogue will not make sense in relation to your previous line. You will now discover that you are an editor! Change whatever words you have to, so that the action flows. Read the other character's dialogue between your two lines and, if need be, incorporate those words or just some of them into your line. Change a statement to a question or the reverse. Add your own words. Don't, however, alter the intent and rewrite the plot severely. If this problem crops up with just about every line, then I suggest you discard this scene.

I have had success creating perfect monologues this way with nine out of ten scenes. If I can do it, so can you.

Don't concern yourself with the length of the piece at this juncture. Just keep creating until the end of the scene or the act. Write down your dialogue on a sheet of paper and read it. Ask yourself if the material has a sense of urgency and if the situation is imbued with passion. If the answer is yes, you have just created a perfect monologue for yourself.

Keep reading it and concentrate on the pacing. Then time your reading. If the monologue is more than two minutes, you have to cut it. Get rid of dialogue that you feel is repetitive and that you can live without. Keep timing it until you've cut it to the two-minute mark or even a few seconds under to give yourself leeway.

If you have not yet read the entire play do so to familiarize yourself with your character and all the events.

Choose someone from life who you feel could be the other character. See this person in your mind's eye as you rehearse and each time you perform the monologue.

Memorize the monologue. Then start making inner-life choices for yourself as character from the day he or she was born to what it is you are fighting for from the other character. Write your character's history and background and all the important events in his or her life leading up to this confrontation. Incorporate what the writer gave to you and add what was not given to you—from *your* head, *your* life, and *your* imagination. Each time you rehearse, begin by reliving your (character's) life from the beginning, reading the character's history that you have written, and when you get to the here and now perform the monologue out loud. You should invest several days on the rehearsals, or even weeks if you are not spending time on it each day. When you feel it is ready to present to a casting director, book an hour with an acting teacher whom you admire and get feedback and instruction.

When you have completed this endeavor, start all over again with a second monologue, and then a third, and then a fourth: two comedic, two dramatic.

At the audition, perform the appropriate monologue(s) for the show you are auditioning for. If the production is a drama, choose your dramatic piece; if it's a lightweight comedy, choose your lightweight comedic piece, and so on. You can see how important it is to have enough monologues to serve you appropriately.

YOUR PERFORMANCE

You will be escorted by an assistant into the audition room or theatre and will stand before the auditors. The auditor(s) will be seated at a desk if you are in an office, or at a table approximately ten to twenty feet in front of you if in a rehearsal hall. If you are in a theatre, the auditors will be in the third row in the orchestra. Hopefully they have found your headshot and résumé among the dozens in front of them. They will greet you and ask what you will be doing for them on that day. Announce the name of your character and the name of the play; say nothing more! If two monologues were requested, announce them both before you begin. Then take a couple of beats and begin your monologue. Casting directors (and all the auditors) don't want you to make eye contact with them once you have begun your monologue; they don't want to be *in* your audition. They really don't want to be the character to whom you are talking, and they don't appreciate being forced into looking at you every moment—at least, that is, in professional auditions where the auditors are more experienced, sensitive, and aware of the actor's process. You will be put off if you are looking at them and see them writing something or talking to an associate or eating a sandwich in your face. Don't be insulted; they don't often break for lunch; it is brought to them to eat during the auditions. They hardly even get a bathroom break!

Place the other character downstage (toward the audience) left or down right above the spectators' heads. Casting directors don't want to see profile, so make sure the other character is not stage right or stage left; *down* is the operative word. When two monologues have been requested, place the character to whom you are talking in the second monologue on the opposite side—if your first character was down left, place your second character down right. Take just a couple of beats between the two monologues.

And how, exactly, should you begin? What cues the auditors to know that you have started acting? During your monologue preparation and rehearsals, a significant part of your time should be spent exploring and rehearsing *whom* you are talking to and *why* you are saying your words to that person. What were the events that lead up to this moment when you begin to speak? What has this person just said or done to you? You should hear those words spoken to you— that hearing is actually the first beat of your monologue— and then respond by beginning your dialogue. (For more on this topic, read *The Perfect Monologue,* by yours truly, Ginger Howard.) If the monologue requires a physical action or gesture at the beginning, you should certainly do it, but it isn't necessary to cue the audience (Attention! I have begun!) by moving. If you have prepared adequately, and really placed your scene partner out there where you can "see" him, your opening moment will be clearly expressed through your body language and the auditors will feel that they have been invited into the world of your monologue at once.

I suggest that you change one item of clothing for the second monologue—take off a scarf, hat, sweater, jacket, remove a long skirt to reveal a shorter one, etc.—and discard the item by simply throwing it on the floor somewhat away from you. You may move about (with definite, energetic movements) but keep the character you are speaking to in place.

Because today is the most important day in your character's life (a choice you must make) and the relationship between the characters is the most important one, do not slouch or wander about aimlessly. Stand tall but have the top half of your body slightly bending forward, toward the person to whom you are talking. Allow energy to emanate from every pore in your being. Connect and communicate with your voice, emotions, and body. Do not look at the floor or at the ceiling. Look at the fourth wall (everything in front of you over the auditors' heads) much of the time; look at the other character at pivotal moments. At the conclusion of your performance, freeze your facial expression and body language for a silent count of five to allow the silent curtain to fall. Then look at the casting director and say a gracious "Thank you." Please do not comment on your own work, either verbally or physically. So many young actors develop the bad habit of shrugging their shoulders when they finish, as if to say, "I'm sorry, that's all I can do." That behavior is just unprofessional and won't win you any sympathy points in the casting competition. No matter what you think of your performance, be gracious, and be proud.

In a professional audition, because keeping to a timetable is paramount, don't be disappointed if they immediately send you on your way without saying a word to you. An abrupt send-off is not indicative of a negative response to your work. You won't be aware of it at that time but it is highly possible that your picture was put on the callback pile. The next time, you will be reading from the script. *Bonne chance!*

PREPARED TWO-CHARACTER SCENES FOR AGENTS

If you are trying to get agents interested in representing you, but you are not presently in a production, where they could see you at work, some agents might invite you to perform a prepared, two-character scene in their offices. Or you could make that suggestion. The other character would be played by an actor/friend of your choosing. Some agents feel that they can better evaluate your talents if they see them displayed in a rehearsed scene. Others prefer cold readings because they feel that if you can present unfamiliar material well, under the stressful conditions of an audition, you can probably rehearse and perform equally well. Most agents will have more confidence in you and will feel more secure when submitting you to casting directors if they know you have studied acting for the audition. Remember, what you do in an audition reflects back on your agent's reputation.

After you have chosen a friend to work on your audition scene with you, you will have to get off book and go through a rehearsal process just as you would for any scripted performance. The choice of the scene is up to you. I can't offer you advice as to what type of scene to choose, but it makes sense that whatever scene you choose to do, your character should be the more interesting of the two, and have more and better lines. I know of many instances where this was not considered by the auditioning actor. The actor-friend somehow ended up with the showcase part and because of a highly visible and impressive reading was offered representation by the agent, while the actor whose audition it was supposed to be got nothing.

Of course, you will always be taking a chance when you do this sort of audition, because your acting partner is inevitably on view. However, you do want to have a reasonably accomplished partner, or you both will look bad. Just give yourself the bigger and better part.

The performance takes place in a small office or, very occasionally, in a slightly larger room used for such purposes. You probably won't have space for elaborate staging, so don't plan on it; don't choose a scene that requires a lot of physicality. Concentrate on your relationship with your partner, and use your body as a prop. You can mime picking up a glass or using a phone, or if you must, bring these hand props. But don't let any physicality interrupt or overshadow your interactions with your partner. The verbal rhythm of your dialogue and the relationship between the two of you is paramount in this type of audition.

You may sit if it is important to the scene, and if there are chairs available to you. You will be in close proximity to the agent; therefore, adjust your vocal projection to accommodate the space. Don't blast them out of their seats. Enjoy this venture; it can be very rewarding.

11.
USING YOUR ACTING INSTRUMENT

ALTHOUGH COMPLEX BLOCKING AND MOVEMENT ARE INAP-
propriate in the audition—because you don't know
the character well enough, because you're not the director,
and because you don't want to move out of camera range—it
is important to remember that the auditioners are observing
all of you. Your face, your body, your emotions, your voice,
and your speech should all be engaged in cleanly and clearly conveying the character. In the next two chapters I will
share with you some of the complaints casting directors have
voiced concerning actors' misuse and disuse of their instruments, and I'll also suggest ways to use all your assets to
their best advantage.

During the reading, actors seem to forget that they have
a face. I know from my observances of young people that so
many of you are devoid of facial expression. I see blankness
everywhere. Was I like that when I was younger? Maybe so.
Read on.

*Almost all the casting directors concurred with the following
statements:*
Please don't exhibit a blank face, responding to absolutely
nothing. We want to see some expression on your faces. Let
there be movement above the neck. Smile when appropriate.
Don't giggle.

I know about this problem only too well. It happens in my classes, too, and drives me crazy. We don't want peripheral acting: face-making, mugging, and gesticulating. This kind of acting is devoid of emotional substance, depth, and honesty. However, be aware that your facial muscles are connected to your emotions.

COMMUNICATING WITH YOUR FACE

Your brain sends a message coursing through you telling you how to react to outside stimuli. You feel it in your guts. Your facial muscles react to your gut feelings. This process occurs within one third of a second.

If you tell me that you are upset with me, I will react with hurt; therefore, my "hurt" muscles on my face will react. I will probably widen my eyes slightly in surprise, hurt, and wonderment as to what I did to upset you. I might frown. That is probably all the movement that will take place. If you tell me that you've just won five million dollars in the lottery, I will probably open my mouth and widen my eyes. If you tell me that your dog died, my "sad" muscles will react because I will feel incredibly sad. If you tell me something happy, my face will respond because that is the way I feel inside. If you tell me something that I absolutely do not believe, my "Oh, come on, you don't actually think I believe you, do you?" muscles will respond.

I am not advising that there be massive activity on your face. But you've *got* to *show* us that you just heard what was being said to you. We don't want a busy face, but we do want an alert face. Acting is reacting. You put your voice where your emotions are, don't you? To *hear* is to *feel* emotion. But don't forget your face; it's hooked into your emotional wiring. Remember, we are listening to you and we are *looking* at you.

It's Human to Smile

There usually is not a stage direction written on the sides to smile. Therefore, it appears that the actor will not take it upon himself or herself to smile even at moments when the character just might do so. In reality, if the actor would happen to be in the midst of the same conversation and event, he just might smile.

In my classes, I ask my students why they didn't smile at what I consider to be highly appropriate opportunities for a smile. Either they missed "the funny," or didn't recognize the absurdity or irony, or they didn't feel warmth toward the other character, or they were not in need, or it didn't occur to them that smiling counted as a facial expression, or they were too nervous to smile, or they simply did not have a commitment to the character; they were reading the lines but they had not done a proper preparation. Therefore, the reading was devoid of humanity.

Don't Giggle Your Focus Away

Giggling comes from nervousness. But it's also from not being in character. It is, after all, the *actor* giggling, not the character. Often when there is funny dialogue or comedic behavior on the part of the other actor reading in the scene, one starts to laugh or giggle, and as I have stated, it is the actor more often than the character he is reading for that is doing the giggling. Yes, it is appropriate to laugh or giggle at funny dialogue, but too many actors get carried away and laugh out of character. They have lost it and auditors and paying audiences alike are able to detect the difference.

If you are one who suffers from chronic problems with giggling, casting directors will have little patience with you. I currently have a student who chronically giggles while doing scenes in class. This person has marvelous qualities and is very much liked by me and everyone, but during the giggling spells, I have no tolerance and I lose it. Giggling has nothing to do with the character and script. If you get the giggles while performing, it is because you are not taking your work seriously. It is a form of embarrassment due to exposing yourself; you are obviously ill at ease in front of people.

Do a little self-analysis while alone. Speak out loud and ask yourself why you giggle. Free-associate (allow your thoughts to naturally emerge—a stream of consciousness) and continue to speak out loud to yourself concerning what is really going on within you when you are giggling. Where does it come from; when did it start; how would you feel if you didn't giggle; does the giggling make you feel good; do you *really* think the situation is funny; how do you feel with people watching you and listening to you; when else do you giggle; etc.; etc.? Make yourself aware that embarking on a professional acting career takes serious work. If you have hang-ups (we *all* have some), address the situation thoroughly and come to some conclusions as to why you giggle. Just addressing the problem will begin to alleviate it.

Articulation Problems and How to Overcome Them

I find that most young people don't speak clearly; I didn't either when I was a teenager. As we mature, some of us, with proper education, and some (not all) who enter the communication world become cognizant of poor speech patterns and we clean up our act in order to be successful. Young people, including young acting students, don't, for the most part, pay any attention to their abysmal speech patterns.

> All the casting directors concurred on the following statements: Don't speak the dialogue so fast that we can't understand you. Make sure your diction is clear. If I can't understand you, I assume an audience won't understand you either.

In my How to Audition classes and, to a much lesser degree, in my Scene Study/Rehearsal Technique classes, I am continually admonishing my students to slow down. They are less nervous in the scene study classes because they have had the luxury of reading the scene several times, getting off book, and completing two or three rehearsals before doing it in class. There are no such luxuries in the audition process; a nerve-wracking experience for too many actors. At the audition, actors read so fast that their work is reduced to line readings. They claim that when they are nervous they talk quickly. The actor becomes a word dispensing machine. No discoveries can be made by the character. Relationship between the characters is negligible. Syllables are dropped. Words are tripped over. The speech pattern sounds like a machine gun rat-a-tat-tatting. Good diction is thrown to the wind. Communication is nonexistent and, therefore, the performance is one tremendous bore and not stage or screen-worthy.

The words on the pages are the least important part of the audition. Don't make the mistake of hurrying from one word to the next. It is not the *saying* of the words that is important. It is the *why* you are saying them and the *how* you are saying them. True, this section of the book is supposed to be about articulation problems, but in reality if you prepare your character properly, many of your speech problems will disappear.

During your preparation for each audition, create your history and background as character. Create all the important events leading up to the confrontation on the pages. Acknowledge what is happening in the here and now on the pages. Create your inner life of what is *not* on the pages. Create the most important relationship you can between the two characters. Create what it is that you are fighting for from the other character.

Your character should always be in need. This does not mean playing victim or a pathetic character (unless you're doing Sophie in the library scene in *Sophie's Choice*). Give each word its due. Use your vowels to help you slow down.

Emphasize words that have emotional significance to you, the *character*. We want a sense of urgency and importance, but not at a galloping pace!

A Practical Prescriptive for Speedy Readers

Get a tape recorder. Record yourself reading dialogue for three minutes. Stop the machine. Rewind. Listen to yourself. Hear how fast you are going. You can't hear yourself when you are inside your head. You can hear yourself when you are on the outside. Correct yourself. Do it again slower. Listen to yourself. Keep self-correcting. Continue with the dialogue. Do this at least fifteen minutes each day. You will correct the problem of reading too fast.

You're Nervous? We're All Nervous!

All actors are nervous to varying degrees during the audition and, indeed, even in classes and during an interview. Nervousness accompanies the actor to the callback, the first rehearsal, all the rehearsals, each shoot, the dress-tech, opening night, and each and every performance. Don't deny it. Acknowledge that it feels as if a large family of monarch butterflies are fluttering in your stomach, that your legs feel like rubber, that your mouth is dry, that your hands are shaking. Incorporate your nervous condition into the scene. Give your nervousness to your character (read my book, *The Perfect Monologue*). Make your reading conversational. Just talk to the other person. Listen and respond. Listen and respond. Listen and respond. Be an aggressive listener. Focus and concentrate on the here and now. Be involved. Shut out everything else from your thoughts.

Listening and Thinking at the Same Time

Regarding reading too slowly, I happily submit that my current and former students' readings at auditions are not slow and lethargic (for the most part).

During the audition, listen to what the other *character* is saying, deal with his words as he is saying them, and respond immediately. There should be no appreciable silence between each character's dialogue.

Reading the dialogue too slowly and waiting several beats before responding immediately reduces the pacing to an agonizingly spiritless, characterless, uninteresting, monotonous hell for the auditors. We can't wait to say "Thank you" and get you out of there. It's like wading through a room knee-high full of molasses. I know that other good acting teachers do not endorse such sluggard readings either.

It appears that actors guilty of this inertia feel that they must take their time in order to convince the auditors that they are taking their character's words oh so damned seriously and that they are thinking actors. Don't think! Do!

Do your thinking during your preparation before the audition. Don't do your preparation in front of us. At best, taking an overly long amount of time to think the words reads as actor self-indulgence. There is no room for self-indulgence for the actor. You must say for each audition you will ever do that, as character, "Today is the most important day in my life. The other character is the most important person in my life. Today is the day that I must change my life and (the other character) is involved in these changes."

We want a sense of urgency. How can you be believable if you read at a snail's pace and if you hesitate before responding? Each time you wait a few beats before responding it becomes a dead spot. (You must have heard the expression "You could drive a truck through the pauses.")

Perhaps in life you might hesitate, but the truth of life does not translate well to the truth of acting. We don't want a slice of life. We want the highlights of life. We don't want the everyday you. We want the highlights of you. We want a character with life and energy.

If the stage directions state that your character is listless or bored or uninterested, or if there are pauses written into the directions on the page, don't fall into the writer's trap. Ignore this kind of stage direction at the audition. Have your character, in your inner life, fight against this inactive and negative state of being. Allow your character's inner dialogue to be, "I don't want to be listless or bored or uninterested." Writers never write about boring characters. Producers never hire boring actors.

12.
USING YOUR VOICE

Your voice must be one that the paying public wants to hear. It is an instrument that can be finely tuned, and it should be just that.

All the casting directors concurred with the following statement:
For theatre, voice should not be small and thin. For camera, voice should be as in a normal conversation.

For those of you who have been instructed by your mothers to speak softly (I wasn't), they didn't do you such a favor if your intentions are to be theatre actors.

I was trained by the legendary Stella Adler. She is the daughter of Sarah and Jacob Adler, famous theatre actors during the latter part of the nineteenth and turn of the twentieth century on the Lower East Side in Manhattan.

Included in their repertoire was Shakespeare performed in Yiddish! The newly arrived, mostly Jewish immigrants from Eastern Europe had a thirst for culture but had not yet mastered the English language, so the Adlers, immigrants themselves and accomplished actors, provided their zealous audience with the majesty of the bard in the spectators' mother tongue.

There was no microphone or sound system in those days. My teacher grew up in this environment and indeed began performing in these productions when she was a teenager. She went on to be a founder of the Group Theatre with Lee Strasberg and Sanford Meisner. Together, they traveled to Russia to meet with and learn from the great Constantine Stanislavski, who had developed his "system." They introduced the Stanislavski System to New York, thus revolutionizing the process of acting throughout North America.

Gone was browbeating, chest thumping, self-indulgence, grandiose gestures, exaggerated elegant speech patterns, posturing, emoting, and being an "ACTOOOOR"! In was naturalistic and honest acting. Actors were taught to discover and utilize their own feelings, sensibilities, vulnerabilities, fears, desires, and life experiences to achieve realism on stage (and in film).

Nevertheless, actors still exercised strong vocal projection so that the audience member sitting in the last row of the top balcony would hear every word. Through the years, even with sound systems, theatre actors continue to project. Actors are miked in musicals, not in straight plays. Theatre actors must be endowed with and sustain a vibrant, absorbing, and appealing voice.

THE DIMINISHMENT OF THE VOCAL INSTRUMENT

In recent years, due to the advent of television, which offers little challenge to acting and vocal abilities, many students have paid little or no attention to honing their vocal skills. Few of them frequent theatre events; they say they can't afford it. Their frame of reference is film and television acting. Of course, there is brilliant acting in some films by *theatre trained actors*. However, when I ask my students what films they have seen, more often than not their reply is an action, horror, or animated film!

Most of my Toronto and Los Angeles students are preparing for a film and television career. The desire for many acting students is to be a movie star. My New York students are more theatre oriented. Statistically and ironically, it is they who will wind up on the big screen earning perhaps not the millions of dollars per film that the muscle boys or a couple of the very funny boys are earning, but, nevertheless, big bucks! (This is not my opinion; this is fact.) Why? Because they understand the importance of years of training. Because they research and seek out the outstanding schools and teachers, investing not less than two and up to six years of intense studying to developing their acting technique, body control, and vocal skills. They may become movie stars but they are also accomplished and powerful actors who *all* started out in theatre!

HAVING WHAT IT TAKES

By the way, regarding those big bucks I mentioned, the aspiring actor who is dedicated to the profession and serious about learning the craft does not enter into this business for the money. And the reality is that most artists do not support themselves solely through their chosen artistic endeavor. I believe that a noble profession is one in which aspirants give no thought to monetary remuneration; that is the world of art and theatre. That is the attitude of the true, emerging artist and actor.

The actors who are revered as North America's finest did not just take an on-camera or improvisation class and, upon completion of the course, book an appointment with a photographer for headshots (with, of course, no professional résumé to accompany the picture) with plans of instantly acquiring an agent. They did not expect to be submitted to casting directors, immediately be granted auditions, and then get the first good part they tried out for! Does this not read as fantasy? Of course. It doesn't happen like this. So why is it that this is the scenario of a substantial amount of would-be actors!?

How do you get to Broadway, Off-Broadway, the Stratford Festival, Shaw Festival, other first-rate theatres throughout North America, and Hollywood films? The same as the person who asks how to get to Carnegie Hall. Practice-practice-practice!

Strengthening the Voice

The student who tells me he or she wants to do theatre pleases me tremendously. However, too often the student has a very thin and weak voice. There will be no theatre acting for this student until steps are taken to strengthen the vocal cords, master breath control, and learn how to use the diaphragm properly.

An astute agent will recognize a small and thin voice immediately and will not submit you for theatre. However, not all agents are so alert and it is disheartening for a casting director to have to waste valuable time with an actor ill-suited for theatre, not because of lack of talent but due to lack of a theatre voice.

Obviously, when doing camera acting, you don't have to be heard in the last row. In a movie house, the audience member in the last row will hear you as well as those in the first row. The sound system is distributed equally throughout the theatre. The actors speak to each other with the awareness that their scene partner is standing next to them or at least in the same room.

However, the exact same level of intensity and passion is required in theatre *and* film auditions. The only difference is voice projection. (Read *Callback* by me, Ginger Howard.)

Working with Accents

As an actor, you want to have a voice that is not only strong, flexible, and emotionally available, you also want clear, articulate speech. When the role calls for it, you want to be able to alter that speech in order to take on the particular character's dialect. Actors who are well-trained have probably learned at least a few regional or foreign accents. But you can do just about any kind of accent requested if you give yourself at least twenty-four hours to work on it.

> *All the casting directors concurred on the following statements:* When an accent is required, please work on it so that when doing it before us it is reasonably accurate. Don't do an accent when one was not asked for.

For a cold (prepared) reading, the character breakdown supplied by the casting director and/or your agent will advise you if an accent is required for the reading. I find that the acting student who demonstrates potential has, among other qualities, a good ear. This means that she or he is curious, fascinated, and interested in the challenge of listening to sounds, ingesting them, and mimicking them. I firmly believe that the most effective way to learn an accent is to spend time with a person who has the accent you are trying to emulate. This, of course, may not be practical since there may be no such people in your life. (But they *are* out there for you to find and listen to and even strike up a conversation with.)

I have heard that some casting directors have informed the actors of the required accent when they arrived at the casting session, not before. The auditors should realize that you need ample time to prepare. If this should occur and you don't feel comfortable about trying the accent, do the audition but ask if they will give you a day or two to work on it and reschedule for another reading with the accent. If they refuse, this is one area where my mandate stating "It is never anyone's fault but your own if you fail at the audition" doesn't ring true. Indeed, the casting director has sabotaged your audition and there is nothing you can do about it. Be assured, this will not occur too often.

The way to get an accent quickly is to rent a film where the characters speak with the one requested by the casting director. I tell actors that you are *renting* the accent also because you won't sustain it longer than a day or so after the audition. View the film; listen carefully to the accent; and at some point into the film, start to speak back to the characters in the accent. It won't be accurate yet, but do it anyway. Then, after listening to more, put the film on pause and repeat or paraphrase the dialogue. Do this repeatedly for a few scenes, rewinding and starting again. Eventually, do your dialogue on the audition sides with the accent. Go back and watch and listen to parts of the film if necessary. Make sure you do this again before you go to the audition. Keep speaking in the accent, including all conversations. *Think* in the accent. Sing a song in the accent. Fall asleep that night speaking and thinking the accent (you might even dream in the accent). Continue talking with the accent on the way to the audition, speaking to the bus driver, the person sitting next to you, the man at the newspaper stand, and the variety store clerk. On the street, ask directions with the accent. Speak to everyone you come in contact with in that accent! Do your preparation in the waiting area using the accent. It will be there during the audition. When you get the callback, repeat this process. Once you get the part, you will be rehearsing daily with the accent.

You may want to record the dialogue into an audiotape so that the video can be returned to the store in time to prevent further charges. If you are flush, then keep the tape for a few days; it's to your advantage to look at the actor as he speaks.

If you take the time for over a period of just one or two days, you will have the requested accent for your audition. You will have prepared like a professional actor should prepare!

You may have seen the audiotapes you can purchase which teach accents, but I like you to see, not just listen to the person talking. Seeing accelerates the learning process.

LEARNING FROM A NATIVE

As I said, the very best way to achieve an accent is to hang out with a person with the required accent. Listen and adopt the accent. You will begin, little by little, to talk as this person does within a very short time. Perhaps as little as fifteen minutes. Mimic to your heart's content. Tape your conversation. All this should be done with the approval of this person.

By the time I was halfway through reading *Angela's Ashes* by Frank McCourt, I was beginning to talk with an Irish brogue just from the rhythm and lilt on those marvelous pages.

Years back, whenever friends or students required an Irish accent, I would invite them to my apartment to talk with my Irish housekeeper, Mrs. Sullivan. Within minutes they would practically sound as if they just got off the boat from Ireland. The funny thing is that she was born in America and had no accent, but she picked it up from her parents and owned it. She could turn it on and off in a beat. And so can you.

WHEN NOT TO USE AN ACCENT

Please do not take it upon yourself to decide that the character you will be auditioning for should, to your way of thinking, have an accent. If the writer and director wanted an accent, they would have given the character the accent and you would have been instructed to do the one requested.

If you honestly feel that the accent is essential, you certainly may offer your opinion *after* you get the part, or at least after your callback when you might diplomatically mention the reasons why you believe the character would talk with an accent. Then ask if they concur with you.

When the character you are auditioning for is English (or whatever) some directors or casting directors will tell you not to bother with the accent for the audition. This can be perplexing for the actor who is perfectly aware that the character is British. Some auditors say they want to find the best actor for the part and then the actor can work on the accent during rehearsals. I personally need to hear at least an attempt at the accent during the audition. I don't want any surprises once we get into rehearsals.

However, if all the characters in the play are British it is not always necessary to hire only those with the accent; a well-spoken American or Canadian cast will do nicely.

Improving Your Speech

I used to wonder why students invest money in acting classes but don't expend one cent on speech classes; now I know why. When I have reproached students whose diction is poor, more often than not their response is that no one, including past acting teachers, had told them that they lacked good diction! These students give me baffled looks. It seems I am the first person to inform them that they are not pronouncing each syllable of every word. I, too, am baffled. Could I really be the first to notice the actors' poor pronunciation?

It appears that the North American educational system does not consider good diction an important factor in the curriculum. As a result, lazy lips are not articulating vowels and consonants; tongues are just lying flat in a mouth that opens wide enough only to masticate a Big Mac. During speech, the mouth is in a lockjaw position.

My answering machine message asks callers to *clearly* state their names and all numbers where they can be reached. Too often, I have to play the message several times attempting to decipher the name and number. I can't tell if they are saying two or three. Unusual names are not spelled out, and when spelled, I can't tell *b* from *d*, *v* from *z*, *f* from *s*, and *p* from *t*. There are times when I simply cannot make out what the name or number is, so there is no return call made by me. When the actors call again and express interest in studying with me, I tell them to take speech classes first and then call me.

Agents are also guilty of not detecting speech flaws when interviewing and auditioning a potential client. However, most legitimate agents will recognize such flaws and will not represent the actor. No writer for film, theatre, or television wants his words spoken by an actor with poor diction. There is no acting career for one with sloppy speech.

There are, of course, many students who are cognizant of the fact that they must speak properly. They are totally aware that proper enunciation is paramount to the actor.

It was always said that the brilliant actor Marlon Brando mumbled. Yes, he certainly did in rehearsals, and he drove his fellow actors crazy. But in performance, his "mumbling" was and is *always* heard and understood by each member of the audience.

If you are not sure about your diction, ask those whom you respect to evaluate it—honestly.

To those with a thick foreign accent, please take classes to strengthen your English skills if it is your intention to perform in North America. I have had numerous calls from would-be students who can barely speak or comprehend English. You will be limited in the types of parts you will be sent up for due to your accent. At the very least, you must be understood and you must have some command of the English language in order to be an actor in North America.

Be honest with yourself. Do you really want to be a professional actor? If so, learn to speak clearly and well. Take speech lessons with a highly recommended speech teacher. Every major city in the United States and Canada offers good ones. Obtain recommendations from acting teachers, the actors' unions, resource centers for actors, or from the local university. In a very small town, the only speech teacher might be on staff at the university. Perhaps this teacher coaches nonmatriculating students also, privately or in a special class. Inquire and, if so, register at once. Acting is skilled labor!

13.

KEEPING IT REAL AND STAYING FOCUSED

AS I HAVE STATED, WITH PROPER TRAINING YOU SHOULD NOT be guilty of inorganic acting. Actors who repeatedly do not get cast are either not giving enough or giving too much. Either way, there is a total lack of honesty to the readings. See what the casting directors have to say and then there will be more from me:

> *Don't* give the words too much emphasis—in other words, don't overact; don't be too dramatic.

I call it inorganic dishonest acting. We have to believe that you are having a conversation, not pontificating.

OVEREMPHASIZING THE TEXT

After watching an actor's reading at the audition, the casting director or director might instruct the actor to "just *talk* to the other character." The auditioners often will allow the actor to repeat the performance because they truly want to give everyone a fair chance. Not necessarily because they are feeling magnanimous, but because they understand that some first readings might not measure up to the level expected, due to nervousness and/or an inaccurate interpretation of the events or relationship on the page. However, don't count on all auditors to give you a second chance. By and large, they will when they recognize potential in the actor even though the reading might be somewhat off.

I believe, as many other casting directors do, that putting too much emphasis on the words is a strong indication that the actor is lacking and is in need of further training.

STAYING IN CHARACTER

The casting director wants to see the character in you consistently—a character based in the text, not another one that you create.

> Don't go in and out of character. Don't do a character that is nothing like what is written.

At times an auditionee will lose it, go blank! Some electrical brain impulse renders one totally out of it. This happens periodically to all of us.

If it happens during a shoot, the scene can be shot again. In a theatre performance, the scene is rendered off-kilter but may soon be forgotten; during a rehearsal, there is little consequence; it can be worked on. In an audition, it is nothing short of disaster for the actor.

Often the actor has not been able to connect with the events or relationship on the page and, therefore, cannot make an inner commitment to the relationships and the dialogue. The actor is detached, as if holding the scene at arm's length.

When you don't comprehend something on the page, create for yourself what you *feel* it might be all about. Be somewhat of a playwright or screenwriter yourself. Your interpretation might differ from the one intended, but at least you will be involved every moment with strong communication. This is much more desirable than being out of it. And there is always the possibility that your interpretation is right on. In fact, I would venture to say that what you come up with, more times than not, will reflect what the writer intended. And if not, it will be assumed that you are right on because your choices were so interesting and strong, perhaps even better than the writer's!

A student of mine was auditioning for a role in a horror movie, and the casting sessions were not very well run. The waiting room was chaotic, it was late in the day, and she had to wait for a long, long time. In addition, the sides that were given to her were not very clear, basically saying something like:

"BOB'S POV:
The woman is infuriated and ad-libs an argument, etc."

The part she was auditioning for was the woman. The character breakdown did say that the woman was a derelict, but there was no dialogue on the sides, and no indication as to what the argument was about.

As she sat there, thinking about the money job she was going to be late for because she was stuck at an audition, she began to grow very frustrated at the way she had been kept waiting and at the inarticulateness of the script. By the time her name was called she had worked herself up into quite a state and was really ready to tell off the director. Instead, she ad-libbed an argument for him, channeling her frustration into quite a lively improvisation. While I wouldn't advise building up that much inner stress and bringing that much fury into an audition if you can help it, I have to tell you, she got the part.

Of course there are those auditionees whose minds simply wander and have poor concentration. I see no reason why such individuals would ever be in the position of auditioning for a professional production of any kind.

Doing a character that is nothing like what is written goes beyond and to a different place than what I just suggested. It happens when the auditionee decides to discard the disposition and attributes of the character created by the writer and invent a whole new being. While it is hard to imagine why anyone would do that, earlier I mentioned the obsession that some actors have with being unique. Intentionally wrongheaded choices may come from an actor's misguided need to show how unique he is. On the other hand, the auditionee may not have a clue as to who that character is!

You've got to display for the auditors that you read the sides and are prepared to service the writer's play/screenplay, which includes presenting the writer's character. Find that character within yourself. Do not make a conscious decision to offer an interpretation that is unrelated to the character on the page.

BEING IN THE MOMENT

Nerves can easily lead to a speed-read of the sides (see chapter 12), and they can also cause you to get ahead of yourself. If you really want to work in the here and now you mustn't anticipate the future. Hear words *as they are spoken.* Don't advertise that you know what the character is about to say. Read the casting director comments and my solutions.

> Don't anticipate the next line instead of listening. Make sure to play the moment.

I know I've repeated this phrase over and over, *but* if you have had sufficient and proper acting training, this should not be a problem. You should have learned to be in the moment and listen and respond; listen and respond; listen and respond.

I don't like to use the word play as a teacher. It's an inorganic word in relation to acting. The character is not playing the moment but is involved in the here and now. You, the character, are very much involved with the person to whom you are talking and the words spoken by both or all of you are important to you and the relationship.

Has it ever happened to you in life that you are talking to someone and her facial expression shows that she sees where you are going and breaks in, interrupting you because she anticipates what you are about to say, and does not allow you to finish? Does this make you feel a little piqued, somewhat annoyed because you were cut off? Such people anticipate what you are about to say and it's very possible they may be wrong. Nevertheless, right or wrong, it's annoying to you and you wish they would just shut up and listen to you and allow you to finish. Don't anticipate; you'll miss what's really going on in the here and now.

On the other hand, you shouldn't stare blankly at your partner, waiting for your turn to speak. Listen to his dialogue; let his words affect you. Remember, a conversation, in the theatre as in life, is built between two people. What you say and how you react must be responsive to and motivated by your partner's words and actions. Listen and discover as you listen.

14.

IS IT COMEDY
OR DRAMA?

I FIND THAT THERE ARE, IN ABUNDANCE, YOUNG ACTORS WHO simply cannot recognize comedic situations. Maybe it has to do with so many inferior sitcoms, stunting comedic appreciation. The following comments are about "funny":

> Know if it is comedy or drama. You've got to have a sense of humor if you want to audition for comedy.

You should be informed by the character breakdown or through your agent whether you will be auditioning for a comedy or drama. Of course, there is a sense of absurdity and irony in all good drama (which actors should be made aware of in their scene study classes).

The auditionee must be prepared when delivering a comedic reading to display a keen sense of comedy *without* playing it for laughs! In comedy you as character must fight extremely hard for what you want from the other character. Without extreme wants and needs, you will not be able to support the big and ultimately funny choices that your character is forced to make.

In the television sitcom *Friends,* two actors who get hearty laughs (maybe you don't appreciate them—comedy is subjective) are Matthew Perry and David Schwimmer. No matter what you may think of the series (I consider the writing to be inferior), notice how these two are always in a state of vulnerability and need, yet the laughs are there. They communicate loud and clear what they are fighting for. They reveal their responses to the words and actions of the other characters through their faces and body language. However, these external responses are the result of their inner feelings. Both of these actors are imbued with a strong sense of humanity; they are behaving like human beings and are not averse to showing it.

RECOGNIZING "THE FUNNY"

You do not have to be a comedic actor to achieve a callback performance at the audition. You have to be a well-trained and accomplished actor to recognize "the funny" on the page. You must understand that in comedy the characters are in the midst of turmoil and conflict just as in a drama, and the characters are not laughing. They are unaware that their situations are imbued with humor. It is the audience that is laughing.

Lighten up! There is humor in drama and drama in humor. If there really is a bankruptcy of humor within you and you don't recognize the absurdity and irony throughout each day of the year and you can't find "the funny" on the pages, then you are really wasting your time and money on acting classes. *All* great dramatic literature contains humor! Perhaps (for some reason) you are not interested in auditioning for comedy but only drama. You will not succeed at your auditions because the irony and absurdity is there on those pages, at least with well-written scripts.

About three-quarters into the last century, I saw *The Indian Wants the Bronx* by Israel Horovitz, starring a new young actor named Al Pacino. He played a menacing young thug, and the entire audience and I were in a cringing mode almost throughout the entire play. He was unpredictable and frightening, yet funny! Part of our laughter might have been precipitated by our fear, but actually, he was so human and embodied so many of the absurdities of human folly that one could not hold back the laughter.

The most successful sitcoms are the ones that deal with and expose the vulnerabilities, frailties, and weaknesses of the characters. They are in the midst of turmoil and are not amused by their situation, but the actors playing them are imbued with a powerful awareness of human impairment accompanied by a vigorous appreciation of the humor in each situation.

15.
A SENSE OF HUMANITY

IF YOU DO NOT PREPARE PROPERLY, THE CHOICES YOU MAKE will not draw the audience to you. We have to "see" your feelings. Here is the way some of the casting directors expressed it:

> There should be a sense of love or warmth in the reading in relation to the other character—in other words, a sense of humanity. There is always love involved in the plot, so the actor should have a sense of romance.

Often an actor in my classes will be in the midst of a reading that deals with a reaching-out-for-love situation, but the actor might as well be talking about the weather or mathematics. When I discuss the absence of love and warmth, stating that it appeared that the actor chose to actually dislike the other character, the actor, who intellectually is fully aware that his or her character is fighting for love, denies that what I stated is so. Indeed, says the actor, the choices made by him included love and the need for the other character.

There are those among us who are unable to expose their vulnerability. You know the kind, those displaying no warmth or congeniality in their discourses and relationships. One who lacks these qualities is categorized as a "cold fish."

LET YOUR VULNERABILITY SHOW

The relationship created by you between the two characters enables the auditors to see your acting range. You *must* make the choice, as character, that the other character is the most important person in your life. You *must be in need* by creating what it is you require from that character, an emotional need that only that character can give to you in the here and now that will enrich your life and that *only* that person can give to you!

In *The Zoo Story*, by Edward Albee, a play studied by most serious acting students, Jerry, an outsider, has designed his own suicide/murder, and Peter, a first class citizen with a proper job and family, has been chosen by Jerry to perform the deed. Jerry confronts Peter in the park, tormenting and provoking him until Peter stabs him with the knife provided by Jerry.

The stakes couldn't be higher. Jerry is fighting, through his harassment, for Peter to get to the point of abhorrence so that he will have no choice but to end Jerry's life. Each actor has a monumental need that is attached to his acting partner. Peter needs to retain his dignity, manhood, and his territorial rights to the park bench upon which they are both sitting. Jerry needs to bring Peter to the boiling point. The inner-life choices made by each actor are literally and figuratively life and death. Once again, there is humor throughout the play, perhaps not in the plot, but in the irony and absurdity of the situation and the dialogue.

You need to make the stakes and the needs of your character *that* important. *You must be willing and able to expose your vulnerabilities.* It's not about if you *can* do it; it's about if you *will* do it! Everyone can; some won't! Those who won't will have no acting career. Well, okay, those endowed with the Hollywood or Madison Avenue standard of beauty (the "hair-teeth-and-bone-structure-school-of-acting face" mentioned earlier) might have a measure of success by being cast by type, not talent, in parts necessitating no more than a minimal amount of acting ability.

TRUE ROMANCE

The Random House Dictionary of the English Language defines *romantic* as: "fanciful; unpractical; unrealistic; romantic ideas; imbued with or dominated by idealism, a desire for adventure, chivalry, etc., characterized by a preoccupation with love or by the idealizing of love or one's beloved; displaying or expressing love or strong affection; ardent; passionate; fervent." All things absent in too many auditions!

Thinking in terms of romance is quite alien to much of the under-forty population. It appears to be an anomaly in acting classes and at auditions. I've been aware of this since the very first acting class I taught and at all the auditions I have conducted.

There was a time when young women caressed layers of fine linens kept in a hope chest while dreaming of their knight in shining armor who would surely appear one day. And when he did, she was coy and he did the courting.

Do we want those times back? No! Of course not. But with the advent of equality for both sexes, romanticism got lost.

Vigorous libidos abound and there is certainly plenty of sexual activity between those of all sexual persuasions. There are singles bars and singles dances and singles ads in magazines and newspapers and singles dating agencies where single men and single women seek partners, companions, lovers (many just for a few hours), and for some, future spouses.

Both sexes are doing the courting. No longer are women waiting for the right man to come along. They are going out all over the place and searching for him if he has not yet appeared in the workplace. More women today hold at least one college degree and are more career oriented than ever before. Women no longer attend college for the sole purpose of finding a husband, as so many did years ago. They no longer just put in the time for the four years until he comes along.

Young people gravitate to large cities where all are strangers. Investing in a romantic relationship can, for many, interfere with the career. Most men and women work long hours and simply have no leisure time. Women are independent and support themselves. They compete with men for jobs. They are equally qualified. They are no longer shrinking violets, especially when they are in a singles bar. They are on equal terms with men on all levels. Some are equal even with physical strength. Women are getting married in their thirties and older. They're having their first children in their late thirties and forties. Women have taken their rightful place!

So, here we are in our fast-paced, equality-based twenty-first century society where people arrange transactions to satisfy appetites and goals instead of pining for knights and dreaming of love. But, when all is said and done, all plays are about love!

Old plays. New plays. Classical plays. Contemporary plays. Comedy and drama. Musical and straight. Satire and melodrama.

Each play deals with the quest for love, the experience of love, the loss of love, or the absence of love. The motivational force behind a character's action is, more times than not, love. There are all kinds of love: familial love, friendship love, love for a stranger who commits an act of kindness, love for a pet, and, of course, romantic love.

In the preparation for your auditions, your character is *always* fighting for love! When it is romantic love, don't leave out the romanticism. Don't be afraid to be unrealistic, fanciful, and unpractical in your choices. Have a desire for adventure, chivalry. Display and express your passion and fervent desire.

There is a very basic acting game usually played with children, but it can be just as appropriate for adults. The teacher asks the class to reach for something on the ceiling. Of course, nobody can reach the ceiling, and the students take halfhearted swipes, in a vaguely upward direction. Then the teacher asks them to imagine something that they really, really want (in real life) is up there, and if they can reach it, they can have it! Lots of skyward leaping results from this instruction.

Do the students reach the ceiling? No (except when there is a basketball player in the class). But they are motivated to make the attempt—they jump with all their might to grab the longed-for prize. In a play or a scene, the playwright might not allow your character to win her heart's desire, but your character must fight for it with all her heart and passion.

MAKING POSITIVE CHOICES

Don't make choices that are going to cause your audience to dislike you. You would be surprised how many times I have said to a student in class after his or her reading, "I don't like you" (meaning the character, of course).

When the actor makes inner-life choices for the character that are devoid of benevolence, let me assure you, it shows in the reading! There are villainous individuals in the world; therefore, there are villainous characters written for theatre and film. But those of you auditioning for and playing these parts must not ever think of yourselves as villains because you as character would never describe yourself as such. Even when you are playing a villain you must make choices imbued with a sense of humanity.

It is not like the old melodramas that I performed at the beginning of my acting career. I performed in a company of actors on a boat turned into a theatre, moored permanently on the Mississippi River in St. Louis. The cast of characters included the handsome suitor, the evil landlord, the kindly old weeping widowed mother, and the young innocent virgin (me). The evil landlord had no redeeming qualities and it was intended that he was to be hated and booed by the audience, who, in fact, brought bags of very ripe tomatoes to be thrown at the villain. Many nights, I had to pick tomato seeds from my ears and hair from the fallout.

Today's soap opera is similar to the melodramas of old. Each character is defined as good, evil, cunning, the bitch, the innocent, etc. There are no opposites. No shades of gray. Just black and white. But in dramatic literature, when you are auditioning for the villain, you must find the redeeming qualities and you must be fighting for love, power, your life, and a happy ending for you, just like any character you will ever audition for and portray. You must not be magnanimously challenged.

16.

GROWING AS AN ACTOR

I F YOU HAVE HAD A MEASURE OF SUCCESS, BEING CAST REPEAT-edly in basically the same sort of character, don't you want to be thought of as an actor with a range? Let's deal with this issue now.

Sid Kozak

There should not be a lack of development. Many actors achieve a certain degree of success and ride on these laurels. They repeatedly do the same kind of roles and do not see the need for growth and new challenges.

Actors should be more flexible. Some work for three or four months and then run dry—are no longer flexible; they now feel like an expert and they are too sure that whatever they do, they will get the part

This happens to actors who have a degree of success in New York, Los Angeles, Toronto, Vancouver, Chicago, Boston, and elsewhere. If you are one of these actors, watch out when you are auditioning for a character diametrically different from the ones you've been auditioning for and doing. Your last good audition and fine performance won't get you the next part. You must recognize, honor, and service the character's particularity.

TAKE RISKS

It is dangerous for an actor to be cocksure of his or her abilities. This attitude will prevent you from stretching and taking risks, and until you are a household name earning millions of dollars a film, you are required to audition for each part. As I said, your last good audition or performance won't get you past the next audition.

I have had several students over the years who were lucky enough to have lengthy runs in hit shows such as *Les Miserables, Miss Saigon, Phantom of the Opera,* and *Cats.* No, they didn't necessarily have star billing, but they were making a good, consistent living doing what they loved. While performing in these shows, these actors registered for classes so that they wouldn't get stuck, so that they would continue to grow as performers. Many of them have told me that since they don't audition when they are in a long-running show, they feel their auditioning skills are getting rusty, and they come to class in order to hone those skills. I applaud those actors because they have no attitude and take developing their craft very seriously.

The greatest actors in the world are constantly concerned that they might have lost it each time they embark on another production. All of them, just like all great artists, believe that they could have done it better. It is a fact that painters have sneaked their paint and brush into museums to retouch or add something to their work. It is said that both Picasso and Dali altered works that were already on public display.

Similarly, great actors never relax about their accomplishments. Each time Anne Bancroft, a fine theatre and film actress, was cast in a play, she worried that she might have lost it, and would let the director and the cast down. Kathryn Cornell, known in her time as "the first lady of theatre," was tortured each time she started rehearsals due to her fear that she might fail in her efforts.

Sir Laurence Olivier never forgave himself for not being able to justify an action in one scene in a Broadway production of John Osborne's *The Entertainer.* I saw this play twice, and I would bet my life's savings that every moment of his performance was magnificently justified!

You have so much to offer as an actor. Face your fears, and always challenge yourself. Don't put limits on yourself. On the practical side, make sure your agent is submitting you for all sorts of characters.

If your agent is submitting you for the same type of character repeatedly, make an appointment with him or her and discuss the kinds of parts you would love to do. Offer to do some readings in the office of parts reflecting the type of characters you want to do. Hear what the agent's objections might be and have a discussion, gently persuading him to take a chance on you. Be diplomatic, but set your sights on the kind of work *you* want to do, the parts *you* want to play. It's bad enough that so many agents and casting directors put actors into a "casting box," defining them as a certain type. Don't do this to yourself. Grow and learn.

17.

THE SMALL PART

E VEN IF YOU ARE ONLY AUDITIONING FOR SMALL PARTS, YOU should approach them with the same level of care and preparation as you would a principal role.

> You might be auditioning for a small part but if your audition is great, you could be bumped up to principal. You might be auditioning for a principal part but might be given sides of a lesser role just to save time. Treat the small role as you would a leading part.

"There are no small parts, only small actors." I've heard this since I started in this business as a child. When you are auditioning for a day player or under five or actor's part (a small part with five lines or less), take it as seriously as if you were auditioning for a leading role. If the character wasn't important, the writer wouldn't have written him or her into the script. Just to show you the kind of attention that writers put into seemingly negligible roles:

Screenwriter Roy Frumkes is presently doing a rewrite of a screenplay (remember, film scripts are often collaborative projects, with more than one author involved) for the director/writer Alejandro Jodorowsky (director of *El Topo*, *The Holy Mountain*, *The Rainbow Thief*, etc.). There's a seemingly insignificant character of a porter in a boardinghouse who has no more than a page of script time. The character in the original script was described as a fat, stuttering man. When Jodorowsky delivered forty minutes of notes for revision to Frumkes, he spent a surprising amount of time on this seemingly unimportant role. "The role of the porter is meaningless as it is now. Let's make it a woman. Let's make it a dwarf woman. Let's make it an ugly dwarf, lesbian woman. She is jealous of the leading lady, who lives on the fifth floor. That is more significant, no?" Like I said, if the character wasn't important to the writer, he or she would not be in the script.

It is exciting to have the opportunity to audition for and do these kinds of parts. The pay is excellent for a minimal amount of time expended by you (in fact, the time spent is so enjoyable you will wish it had taken longer). You will be treated royally by everyone on the production crew. You will be given a dressing room, you will be given your special wardrobe, you will report to makeup where the star might very well be in the chair next to you, you will be offered the same food as the principals and stars, and you will be escorted or driven to the soundstage or location of the shoot.

Working Your Way Up

In the beginning of your career, it is these types of auditions that you probably will be sent up for until your résumé displays a fair amount of work. Most agents don't submit clients with a minimal amount of experience for principal parts because most casting directors are not open to seeing green actors for anything beyond small parts. You have to prove yourself. Be thankful that you are getting where you want to be—one step at a time.

Don't be surprised, however, if you recognize a working actor auditioning for these parts. The competition is fierce and when an actor is between principal parts, he or she will gladly audition for the small parts and appreciate the experience and the money.

When you audition for a small part, be aware that if you give a superb reading (and auditors recognize one no matter how small the part is) and they have not found anyone suitable for a bigger part, they will often give you a go at it.

18.
THANK YOU. NEXT.

WHAT YOU SAY AND DO AFTER THE READING IS PART OF THE audition and is revealing about who you are. There are do's and don't's for you to be aware of. In the event that you are not cognizant of what they are, they are presented here with casting directors' comments.

> Hold the character or focus until I call cut. After your reading, don't ask us when the callbacks are. After your audition, don't ask if you can hang out and watch other actors audition. Don't exhibit frustration and disappointment and make excuses for why you feel you gave a bad audition. Audition etiquette and attitude are very important. Actors should never walk into a room with an excuse for why they are not going to do a good job or apologize after a read. Don't blame your agent for everything.

The last thing casting directors want to hear from an auditionee is why the reading is poor. Can you imagine what it is like for them to eagerly await each actor, hoping for a splendid reading and being forewarned not to expect one!

NO BLAMING OTHERS

You are only fooling yourself if you put the blame on others for your failures. Most failure occurs when you *allow* someone or something to sabotage your efforts. Take responsibility for any failures; this is the first step in diminishing them.

If you walk in and announce that you will not be giving a good reading for whatever your reasons are, most casting directors, including myself, will invite you to leave immediately. We would believe you and would be grateful to you for prewarning us. We don't want to deliberately subject ourselves to a poor reading.

I cannot believe that an actor would actually behave this way. Don't ever make excuses to the casting director. If you haven't been able to prepare for the reading or you are in the midst of some personal turmoil, either ask if you can be rescheduled or give the best ice-cold reading you can give with no excuses before or after.

Be realistic. When you fail at the audition, it is *never* anybody's fault but your own. Your agent might not have provided you with the proper information or might have contacted you about the audition at the last minute and so on and so forth. The bottom line is no matter what the variances are, you as a professional have to pull it off. Blaming your agent doesn't cut it for the casting director. Whatever the problem is, it is between you and your agent.

The best thing you can do when you are aware that the performance you just gave was less than what you feel it should have been is to simply leave. Some actors who are cognizant of the fact that the reading was poor will automatically feel the need to try to justify a poor reading—in other words, to make excuses to the auditors. The auditors don't want excuses! They want a good reading!

No Apologizing

Apologies for a poor reading are not welcomed by casting directors. It is assumed by them that you didn't consider your audition seriously enough and you allowed life's disturbances to take precedent. The bottom line is that they don't care why you gave a bad reading. They were hoping for a good reading and they are now disappointed. They thrive on good readings!

Despite the fact that, as previously stated, apologies for a poor reading are not welcomed by the casting directors, when an actor gives a poor reading accompanied by a cavalier attitude, it will unquestionably be the actor's last one for that casting director. At least be pleasant to one who is in a position to advance your career. Behave decently to your fellow living beings and exhibit a sense of humanity.

HOLDING THE MOMENT

When you have come to the end of your reading, stay in character, keeping the same expression on your face for a silent slow count of five. If the casting director is going to call "cut," chances are it will be within those five beats. If by then the call hasn't been made, you may then break character. Not all casting directors call "cut." This call is usually made by the director during the shoot.

WE'LL CALL YOU

In my experience as casting director, the actors who ask when the callbacks will be held are, by and large, the ones who have read badly. We are amazed at their presumption and that they are so unrealistic and out of touch with what they have just presented. The casting director or director then must answer the actor. At this point the callback schedule is an inappropriate issue, just as it is inappropriate for the actor to ask. The well trained, serious actor hopes to get a callback but, for the most part, has no inkling whether or not there will be one and, indeed, is concerned that there won't be one.

YOU ARE NOT THE AUDIENCE

Please do not ask if you may hang out and watch other actors audition. In a professionally run audition, the answer will always be a resounding no! The audition is conducted by and witnessed by the production staff only. Anyone else is considered an intruder.

For an amateur production, anything goes. There is, of course, a protocol there, also, but usually it is much more casually run than a professional casting session. You certainly may ask even though you might be refused. You might want to ask if you can be of assistance in some way, and by helping out, you will have the opportunity to view the auditions. You've got nothing to lose and perhaps something to learn; but remember, this is for amateur productions only!

MAINTAIN A POSITIVE ATTITUDE

Juli-Ann Kay of Ross Clydesdale Casting stated:

> If their attitude is good, I will erase the tape and let them do it a second time.

Many casting directors will do the same. Be pleasant, give no excuses, keep your frustration and disappointment at a minimal level, and you certainly may ask to do it over again. You have nothing to lose. If the casting director sees some potential in your work and you display a positive and pleasant attitude, chances are you will be allowed to do a second reading. If not, be gracious and, with all the dignity you can muster, leave.

19.
THE CALLBACK

IF YOU GAVE A FIRST WINNING AUDITION THERE IS NO EXCUSE for not giving a second one at the callback. Yet actors are still failing at their callbacks. See what the casting directors have to say and then I will go over the callback situation in detail.

DEBORAH BARYLSKI

Don't change the audition (the choices or point of view, etc.) between the first audition and the callback. Actors don't seem to realize that the reason they get callbacks is *because of their first performance,* and then they come in and change the audition *without being asked to do so.* It makes everyone nervous. Repeat the work. Remember what you did the first time. Don't give us a reason to wonder, "Will they try being creative when I'm on a deadline and going into overtime?"

All the casting directors concurred on the following statements: We are excited about what you did at the audition and then disappointed when you give an awful reading at the callbacks. It's the same material you did the first time; just repeat it. You've got to remember everything about the first time. I've told the director who was not at the first audition about a wonderful actor I auditioned. Then at the callback he does a dreadful reading and the director looks at me wondering if I know what I am doing. It really is so simple. All we expect of them is to just repeat what they did the first time.

Actors who fail at their callbacks do so because they don't prepare for them in the first place. A callback is your second audition for the production, which means that you gave a winning audition the first time and you are being called back to be seen again. You are being seriously considered for the part.

CREATIVE VISUALIZATION

There is a preponderance of dull and lifeless work done at callbacks that simply should not occur. Powerful, incisive, and profound choices at the first audition were obviously made, resulting in a performance deserving of a callback, most likely employing some creative visualization, whether the actor realized it or not (working actors *do* creatively visualize the future of the character at the audition, rehearsals, and performances). The application of this tool adds vivacity and life to the readings.

In creative visualization, there are no obstacles, losses, or defeats. It's fantasy time all the way. You project your future exactly as you want it to be with no detours, boundaries, or constraints. This applies not only to your choices for the characters but to choices regarding your personal goals as an actor.

Add to your acting choices for your character the future that you as character wish for. Incorporate in your preparation for your character your own personal dreams and desires. Make these choices be ones that you personally aspire to. You've already been creating a history and background for your character, dealing with the here and now and what you are fighting for from the other character. Now see the future for your character, which, of course, is positive and fulfilling. (We always fight for happy endings in life, don't we?)

SUSTAINING A PERFORMANCE

At the callback you must demonstrate to the auditors that you can sustain your performance and that your first one wasn't a fluke! In fact, too many actors fail at the callback because of poor preparation or, in most cases, no preparation at all. The time to prepare for the callback is at the *first* audition. There are two steps to take in preparation. First, when you have read the sides carefully and have made your inner-life choices, it is time to do a little creative visualization.

In creative visualization, we intentionally call into being that which evolves from our thoughts, imagination, wishes, and fantasies (read my book, *Callback*).

After working on creating the history and background of the character, concentrate on important events leading up to the confrontation in the dialogue on the audition sides. Then work on the here and now, meaning what is being said by the characters, the action taking place, and also what is *not* being said. Finally, work on the future, which must exist in and emanate from the mind of the actor. If the actor, through creative visualization and projection, is making choices— what I think of as all-important, life-and-death choices for the character's future, based on the *actor's* very personal fantasies, visions, imagery, and dreams—during the preparation, the performance becomes more powerful, alive, and formidable. The actor, because of the higher stakes and added stimulation, communicates more and, therefore, is more appealing and exciting to watch and listen to. The actor must have a commitment to and an investment in the future welfare of the character he is auditioning for.

DON'T PANIC! TAKE NOTES

When actors get the phone call saying, "You got a callback," the first reaction is joy. But the second one is panic. Let's keep the first one and discard the second one.

The reason actors panic is because they can't remember what they did at the first audition and/or they feel they must improve their performance at the callback. These are the reasons why actors fail. *Repeat! Do not improve!* They loved what you did the first time, which is precisely why you are getting the callback. It is important for you to remember what went on the first time. Therefore, I suggest that you bring a notebook and pen to all auditions. This is the second step in preparing for the callback. At the conclusion of your audition, sit in the waiting area or someplace nearby and write the entire scene you just did, paraphrasing. Don't use the writer's dialogue exclusively. Write about what just transpired on those pages in your own words. Write how you as character feel about the other character, how he or she treats you, what the event is, and what you are fighting for from that person. Keep writing; freeassociate. (Just write what pops up into your mind; don't sit and think.) This activity should take you approximately five to ten minutes. When there is nothing left to write, start another paragraph and now write as actor and evaluate what you just did. Did you feel you gave a good reading? Why? Not so good? Why? Then write down what you wore, including undergarments, which scent you wore, etc. Before you go to sleep that night, read the pages, and then put them in your night drawer.

A week or a month later (in some cases four months; it's happened to me), when you get the call, you may indulge in the feeling of joy but as you are about to panic, stop and remember those pages in your drawer. Read them, and you will be brought back to the scene and what you did the first time. Go to your callback wearing the same outfit and scent with assurance that they love you, and give them what you gave the first time!

Break a leg.

20.
CASTING DIRECTORS ARE HUMAN TOO

BECAUSE CASTING DIRECTORS ARE THE GATEKEEPERS STANDing between the actor and the job, actors sometimes ascribe a lot of power to them. At times this makes it difficult for actors to remember that casting directors are just people who are doing their jobs, that they are human beings with lives, loves, families, outside interests, etc. It is important to recall that casting directors deserve the same common courtesy that all of mankind deserves.

The following words, from Toronto casting director Shasta Lutz of Jigsaw Casting, elaborate on the subject of social etiquette:

> I was at an intimate dinner with my boyfriend at a restaurant the other night. We're talking about our future, catching a nice buzz from the wine, when I hear, "Excuse me, are you a casting director?"
>
> "Not tonight," I reply.
>
> He got the hint, or so I thought, when he reappears with a fellow actor, "Excuse me, didn't you audition my chin this afternoon?" (A singing chin commercial; don't ask.)
>
> "Yes, maybe," I reply, but to be honest I don't recall the chin and she didn't get the job, which made me feel kind of guilty. . . . She also didn't even know who she was auditioning for—my name, that is. Leave us alone or at least send over a glass of what I'm drinking if you are going to interrupt me.

On the other hand, if we're at an event or your agency's Christmas party and you got a big paying commercial through me and it was fun, say hello because, more than likely, I'll remember you, because my pocket was padded, too. Please introduce yourself because standing there grinning while I rack my brain is easily avoided; it's also easier to introduce you with proper pronunciation to the hot director who's using me to cast his/her next project.

A good agent who doesn't submit you for every single role helps because I get tired of seeing your face before I've met you. How can you be perfect for this beer-drinking alternative type and be trying out for the accountant as well? Persistence, more training. I certainly like to be invited to a good performance, but remember: You only have the opportunity to meet someone once. Use your judgment when your role is small or if the play sucks. Even if you're good and the play stinks, wait to invite us out or we'll hate you, because whomever we took to the show will hate us for wasting their time.

Here are just a few more comments from the gatekeepers, to help you understand their point of view:

We need you as much as you need us. I know it can be intimidating or nerve-racking in front of total strangers, because unless they're repeat clients, casting directors are in a room of people we've never met, account people, etc. We are auditioning as well! Remember, we are on your side. We look good if you look/act well.

Even though we all fish from the same pond, we all use a different hook.

A client doesn't know what they want until it walks through the door.

When you give a good audition, we love you madly! We may not show it. But believe that this is true.

We eagerly wait for each actor, hoping that he or she will be "the one."

We are servicing our directors. When we screen you at the first audition and call you back to audition for the director, it's almost as if we are auditioning for him or her, too. You make us look and feel good when you're good. Our directors love us and want to hire us over and over.

There are some directors who give the casting director credit for an actor's great performance. It's as if they feel we had something to do with the work. It doesn't make sense, but, hey, who's complaining?

You have the power to make or break my day.

You must be mad to want to be an actor, so accept that fact. You are crazy!

21.
THE ACTING GENE

THE "RANDOM HOUSE WEBSTER'S DICTIONARY" DEFINES A gene as "the unit of heredity transmitted in the chromosome that, partially through interaction with other genes, controls the development of hereditary character."

This definition begs the question: How do you get an elephant out of the theatre? The answer? You can't if it's in his blood.

We know that one's parents or grandparents need not have been endowed with a proficiency in acting—or, for that matter, a proclivity for any of the arts—to generate artistic offspring. But perhaps, hidden in the chromosome, there was some sort of transmission, some sort of interaction with other genes that played a part in the development of hereditary character leading to the arts, as if you were born to act, to paint, to create. An inherent instinct.

On occasion, I see raw potential when observing a student's first scene in class. These are students who are able to expose their vulnerabilities, warts and all, and to convey emotional reach-out, emotional action, a commitment to the character and to the relationship, and a fearlessness of taking risks and being wrong. In those auditions, traits beyond what are written for the character are exposed and what we end up seeing are human beings imbued with a strong life force in the midst of conflict, communicating verbally and emotionally with each other. Due to the fact that the actor is not cognizant of the script beyond those few pages, has had no rehearsals, no direction, and just his or her own preparation for the audition, I know I am in the presence of one who has "the acting gene." (Of course, there are those who show no potential on first viewing—or second or third—but oh, what happens eventually during the class! Suddenly there is a breakthrough and the stu-dent comes through with a powerful reading. I call these students "slow starters.")

Many actors felt drawn to acting at a very young age and participated in plays from grade school through high school. When I was in the third grade, at P.S. 177 in Brooklyn, I was cast as a carrot. My very first part! The play was about victory gardens. My mother sewed an orange carrot costume for me. My dialogue was, "I am a carrot. I am orange and I taste very good and I am very healthy to eat." The audience, made up of the student body, teachers and mothers, applauded. For me! Applause! My first dose of exaltation. And then when I was ten, I wrote a play about a princess, prince, king, queen and a witch. We spread the word in the neighborhood that the admission fee was a large safety pin. We had blankets to pin to the clothesline, but we were in need of those safety pins: as each audience member would arrive and donate the pin, the "curtain" would be assembled. Sadly, on the day of the performance I got the mumps and had to relinquish my part. The show took place without me, with another young girl basking in my spotlight. I sat at our kitchen window, which looked out onto the backyard "stage," and watched my play being performed without me, hot tears streaming down my puffy face.

How old were you when you decided that you wanted to be an actor? Were you a child or a young adult? What was the response from your parents? Did they honor your wishes and take you to a teacher who works with youngsters? If they got encouragement from the teacher, did they follow through by taking pictures of you and then submitting the pictures to agents? Did they approve of your wishes and encourage you along the way? Or, in high school, did they oppose your desire and strongly advise (indeed, demand) that you study a back-up curriculum in college, so that in the event that you didn't become successful as an actor you would have something to fall back on? Surely this sounds like practical and pragmatic advice—and it is. There is only one thing wrong with it: under these conditions, statistically, you probably will not wind up supporting yourself as an actor.

Many acting students who have studied with me and with other professional acting teachers have complied with their parents' wishes to attend college not majoring in theatre, to keep peace in the family. I am all for a four-year college education, but for those who seriously aspire to have a career as an actor, to be sure, this advice can backfire unless your major is theatre. Parents always fear that their son or daughter might not make it as an actor. This is pragmatic, but negative, thinking, because their good intentions serve to manipulate your trust in yourself.

Assuming that you might not succeed as an actor is counter-productive thinking, and in itself is sabotaging your future as an actor. In reality, you might not make it as an actor. Even with a diploma from a three- or four-year college acting program, you are still eligible to be a waiter, a job that will be readily available (unlike acting). The sad truth is that one per cent of acting students are eventually able to support themselves as actors. These working actors fall into two categories: those with the "hair, teeth and bone structure acting face," and those with genuine talent. Acting is skilled labor. You might have an innate sense of the human condition, but technique and discipline have to be developed to accompany cognition and observation.

If you comply with your parents' wishes, of course you might still eventually become a working actor by taking professional acting classes during the summer months in college and after graduation. However, by making acting your major and then augmenting your studies with professional classes during the summer months and after graduation, your commitment will pay off much more effectively.

Let me reiterate: *acting is skilled labor*. Be aware that the actor who is cast in professional productions and whose work is admired by the theatre or film patrons has invested the required hours of instruction to develop acting strengths. An accomplished actor has learned how to live the emotional stage/screen life; how to create a strong life force; how to gain confidence; how to make life and death choices; how to abolish fear of risk taking; how to create relationships with other characters; how to develop character; how to tap into his/her life to embellish, physicalize and personalize; how to develop communication skills; how to deal with nervousness; how to delve into script analysis in order to service the writer's script; how to rehearse; how to own the part; how to implement creative visualization; how to be open to improvisation; plus so much more.

The finest actors appearing on stage and screen throughout the world invest in years of study before embarking on the harrowing audition process. These are the actors who did not achieve stardom because of their "hair, teeth and bone structure acting face." The great ones—those who have an awareness of human frailties and strengths and can dish out a healthy dose of empathy—are hired because of talent not type. They expose their vulnerabilities, warts and all, and are not afraid of making fools of themselves. (If one is not fearful of looking like a fool, one will not be looked upon as a fool.) These actors develop because of an innate intelligence and sense of humanity. They are highly curious about the behavior of humans and animals, with all the peculiarities, idiosyncrasies, quirks and mannerisms inherent therein. They have impeccable instincts—"the acting gene"—and possession of an innate awareness of human behavioral process beyond their own. They are acting "human," therefore we don't see the "acting."

With very little exception, the finest actors performing in film started out on the stage. Most television and film scripts do not present an enormous challenge to the actor, so many of these actors, throughout their career, return occasionally to the stage. They need the continuity of action, the live performance, a live theatre audience, the challenge and pleasure of emoting literate scripts for adult minds, and they are willing to sacrifice a potentially high celluloid salary (where large sums of studio cash flow from virtual fountains) for this in-the-flesh pleasure. It's worth it to them, because on stage is where one fully experiences the thrill of acting.

22.
BEING REALISTIC/
FALSE EXPECTATIONS

OVER THE LAST SEVERAL YEARS IT HAS BECOME APPARENT to me and to many acting teachers throughout North America that a preponderance of acting students' level of cognizance and mental skills has "gone missing"! The situation has increasingly worsened over the past few years.

I blame this dilemma on the public school system. It seems to me that teachers are instructed to pass everyone and get them out, and therefore neglect to correct problems such as bad grammar and abysmal English-language skills. Furthermore, students are not instructed to read the classics and hold discussions about great authors and great minds, a practice that facilitates an expanded use of language; and they do not avail themselves of professional theatre (admittedly the price of a ticket can be out of reach for most young people). When they register for instruction with me, I must correct their grammar continuously. I tell them I am allergic to incorrect grammar and will break out in emotional hives—and they believe me! It is simply unacceptable in the theatre world not to express oneself properly. As a matter of fact, I correct bad grammar on the phone to those calling me for information about my classes. Some are shocked by my reprimands, but at least they know what they are in for if they study with me.

By the time students have reached their senior year in high school, many have not yet considered a career in acting, and they may or may not have performed in a play in school. More often than not they had little or nothing to do with their school's drama department (that is, if their school even had one).The majority of young people attend action films, not character and relationship films showcasing the finest actors in North America and England; and they are devotees of the idiot box, observing individuals eating disgusting creatures for cash and watching mindless sit-coms. As a result, we have a new generation each year of undereducated, poorly informed, weak-minded young people. And this is America's and Canada's future!

Of course there are those who excel in their studies and go on to higher education and become doctors, lawyers, professionals and, yes, actors! These aspiring actors attend three- or four-year programs at universities and colleges, do well academically, major in theatre and choose to have a career in acting. Many of these students pursue further studies with professional acting teachers, during summer break or after graduation, before embarking on agent auditions. The reality in the professional acting world is that some actors, even working actors who have studied seriously over a period of years, take an occasional class throughout their career; and some of the greatest actors working today studied at least three to eight years before their first professional performance.

Acting students take note: 1) One week is not long enough to train the actor in auditioning skills; 2) A teacher should have personal experience in the casting of productions in order to teach acting for the audition. I have been a guest teacher in several colleges and among the classes I offer is a basic acting class and an acting for the audition class, which is, indeed, an in-depth acting class. I work with each student on his/her level.

The climate has changed over the years for independent acting teachers. We get graduates (or sometimes drop-outs) who don't know what they want to do with their lives and possess the skills only to wait tables or perhaps type (slowly), and so they say, "Hey! I know what! I'll be an actor!" Lord, preserve us— those are the kind of students registering with independent acting teachers. Not all, mind you, but a vast number of registered students in each class every semester fall into this unfortunate category. They know that actors have head shots, so even before their first class begins they have already chosen a photographer (usually a cheap, inferior one). This young, ill-informed, naïve person is now ready for his/her fabulous career in acting where tons of money will be made!!! These individuals feel, oh, so important and glamorous with their professional head shot, which, sadly, will most likely function only to fill a section of a drawer. The serious acting student knows that head shots should not be taken until the conclusion of all acting training.

The reality for some students eventually sets in—with a thud! Many of them cannot accept criticism in class. They become defensive and at times offensive to the teacher, because they are embarrassed when given feedback that doesn't pump up their egos. Not wanting to be criticized, they feel that the teacher is picking on them for no reason. Actually, they do begin to realize that they are in over their heads and start to feel defeated, and the only way they can handle this is to lash out in anger. Eventually they drop out of the class.

I am writing this as an advance warning to you, dear reader: Please be honest with yourself and admit if you fall into this category, because there will be no acting career for you! The truth hurts, but nevertheless it is the truth.

One does not attend acting classes to "learn *how* to act"! Acting classes are for those who already have a passion for and innate sense of identification with the characters and dialogue on the pages, on stages and in films. *Acting teachers do not teach students how to act!* We hone your innate, *already-existing* acting skills! We honor what you bring to us and assist you to build from there. We push. We provoke. We encourage. We cause you to think, to feel, to dream, to expand your world and your fantasies. We want results eventually, but not until the student lives through the process. This process leads to the result, a most rewarding and exhilarating place to be.

You must bring the foundation. Passion! Awareness! A thirst for study and learning! Curiosity. Flexibility. A totally open mind. An inborn ear for hearing—and a heart for feeling—how people express themselves and struggle internally. A powerful curiosity about human behavior patterns. An overwhelming desire to act for the love of acting, not for the money. (If it is money you think you will reap, get real! In the end, you will have wasted hundreds, possible thousands, of dollars on acting classes.) The more a student brings to me, the more I can contribute to the student. That is where the glory and great rewards are in teaching a noble profession such as acting. It takes dedication and genuine love and nothing less than a fervent passion for theatre.

I advise my students to see as many plays as they can. It's a learning process for the acting student, as well as a highly enjoyable experience (well, most of the time). Throughout my adult life, I have seen practically every play produced on and off Broadway, many several times: *Torch Song Trilogy*, six times, and I joyously cried at the end of each performance; *Fiddler on the Roof,* four times; *West Side Story*, four times; *Guys and Dolls*, three times; *La Cage Aux Folles*, three times; different productions of *Picnic* three times; *Who's Afraid of Virginia Woolf?*, four times; *Death of a Salesman*, three times; *Long Day's Journey Into Night*, three times; *House of Blue Leaves*, three times; *Waiting for Godot*, three times; *Hedda Gabler*, three times; and the list goes on.

23.
CURIOSITY

RECENTLY, ON ONE OF MY SEVERAL TRIPS THROUGHOUT THE year to conduct "How to Audition" workshops throughout America and Canada, I sat next to a gentleman on a flight from Toronto to Dallas. As I am prone to do, I initiated the conversation by asking him where he was from. He told me and then offered additional information about his life which included his marriage, children, profession (a dull one), reason for travel, additions being added to his home, the make of his car, the make of his wife's car, how he met her, the family's upcoming trip to Hawaii, and assorted other tidbits. He disclosed much more than I bargained for, but I graciously listened with a polite smile (at least I think it was polite) which after over twenty minutes was becoming a strain on my facial muscles.

When he finished his soliloquy there was thunderous silence emanating from him. I am not prone to disclose intimate details to strangers about my life, but I have no compunction about sharing mundane details on a three hour flight if asked. Actually, I enjoy creating imaginary stories just to entertain myself, doing no harm to the listener, embellishing my own tidbits to liven up the trip. However this very pleasant man did not ask me one question about myself! He apparently had no interest in my existence with the exception of my functioning as a listening post.

He possessed no *curiosity*!

Perhaps, I thought, he felt it would be rude to ask, despite the fact that he offered much information about his life. No, I realized, he lacked curiosity. I thought, well, he's not an actor so he doesn't have to have an inquisitive nature. This, in essence, is one of the reasons why I find too many individuals not in the theatre world to be rather dull company. They talk about themselves and have little interest in others. They lack curiosity.

Writers are of a curious nature, at least published writers. They, too, must be alert to human behavior patterns, attitudes of others, personal sensitivities, life experiences, observations of other minds and varied thought processes. Painters observe life around them. They are curious about the details and configurations of faces, flowers, trees, buildings—everything on the earth and in the sky. They look, and indeed they truly see, and then interpret what they see.

I regret to say that a large number of acting students, including those who study with me, are lacking a curious nature. An acting student must not be self-absorbed. As I say to my students: if you are not interested, you will not be interesting. An actor must be curious! An actor must observe, study, listen, inquire and probe into the patterns of people and animals, their behaviors and experiences. Working actors have it. Actors universally admired are of a curious nature.

If you have been taught by your mother that it is not polite to ask questions or probe into other's lives, leave that lesson behind. Lose it! Watch and observe human behavior patterns, listen, ask questions and suck up anything you can about the behavior of others. Keep it all on file in your head. You will be auditioning for and playing characters that are far removed from yourself, and you must find those characters within you. You are actually a filing cabinet; or, I suppose these days, a living and breathing computer. Be observant when in the midst of others. Watch and listen. This is part of your homework as an acting student. Observe how people respond to various situations, verbally and non-verbally. Observe body language—a potent language! Study people around you on the bus, subway, on the street, everywhere.

And when on a plane, at least say hello to the person sitting next to you.

24.

ACTORS' AUDITION MISHAPS: IN THEIR OWN WORDS

ALMOST ALL ACTORS HAVE A STORY TO TELL ABOUT MAKING a fool of themselves at an audition. The following stories are generously provided by those who can now look back and laugh at themselves and the embarrassing experience. You might have one or two yourself. Or if you are about to embark on auditioning, be aware that it happens to just about all of us. Although you might be mortified at the time, you will one day look back and laugh. I offer the first saga and disclose and share with you my own embarrassing experience. Yes, the experts have them, too. I'm only human. As my father used to say, "We all make mistakes. That's why they put erasers on pencils."

> I was auditioning for a commercial and was placed behind a large table on which were metal pots, pans, roasting pans, measuring cups, pitchers, and bowls. I was to play a housewife in the kitchen preparing to mix ingredients for cake baking, but who was flustered and frustrated over this endeavor. I was instructed to use the props in such a way that they would fall out of my hands onto the table and bang into each other, causing a lot of noise and, in general, making a racket. My face was to reflect my frustration. There was no dialogue.

I did my slate and began my audition. I was banging and dropping and crashing each prop into each other and I really was getting into it more and more and actually letting off some steam.

On that day I was wearing my clunky shoes, the kind workmen wear. Well, somehow one of my feet tripped the other and in the midst of the racket I was making, I suddenly disappeared from sight and from the camera range. I fell to the floor. One moment I was there, and the next, I was gone! I was able to visualize from the auditor's point of view this sight and how funny it must have looked. I burst into laughter while lying on the floor, and I could not, for the life of me, stop laughing or get up. The casting director ran to me, looking at me in horror, which made me laugh all the more from the expression on his face. When I was finally able to compose myself, I got up, assuring him that I was not hurt. I left and when entering the waiting area and seeing all the actors, I burst into laughter again (I have a large laugh). It continued as I left the building and was walking down the street. I didn't dare get on a bus in that condition. I walked home, laughing all the way.

The following day I faxed the casting director apologizing for my behavior. No, I didn't get the part.

X X X

I had taken some vitamins in the waiting area, one of which was a capsule. I swallowed them without benefit of water. Several minutes later, I was summoned into the audition studio. I started my slate and as I spoke, a stream of white powder blew out of my nose and mouth. The casting director's face reflected shock. It didn't register with me that the cause was the capsule. I just stood there, stupefied. When I opened my mouth again to speak, more of the white stuff blew out. The casting director suggested that I leave immediately, assuming, of course, that I had taken an illegal substance. I explained about the vitamins and that the powder was from the capsule, all the while, of course, with white powder being purged from my nostrils and mouth. I begged her to believe me, but she insisted that I leave.

The capsule had melted in my throat and the contents just came billowing out of me; I wanted to fall through a hole in the floor. I explained what had happened to the monitor in the waiting room and begged her to relay this to the casting director. She must have done this because I did get to audition for that casting director after that incident. All was forgiven. Now I carry bottled water with me.

X X X

I was auditioning for a play when suddenly, during my reading, the casting director and director let out a scream, jumped out of their seats, and ran for the door.

I stopped the reading and stood there frozen, thinking my reading could not have been that bad. Is this their way of displaying rejection of an actor? I thought their attitude was not very professional. They could have just stopped me, thanked me, and sent me on my way.

Then I saw a movement on the floor in front of me. It was a mouse cavorting, and it obviously was a frightening sight to them. I love animals so I was not affected as they were. I spoke to it and guided it away from the center of the room, hoping to get it to a small enclosure so that it could protect itself from these crazy people. They finally came back and I continued the reading, fearful that at any minute, the mouse would resurface.

X X X

When I first started to audition years ago, I got it into my head that I gave the best readings if I ran in to start the reading instead of standing in place. These auditions were mostly for community theatre. The auditors would oblige me. Once when I was given permission to run in, I went all the way out into the street, wetting myself down from a water bottle. I ran in and as I got to the marker on the floor, I yelled out, "I'm sorry I'm late." This line was not in the script. Everybody laughed except me. The director must have assumed I was crazy, and I don't blame him. I stopped running in from then on.

꒰ ꒰ ꒰

I was instructed by the casting director to start the audition sitting down and midway through to get up. I sat with my legs crossed and proceeded with the reading. When I reached the place where I was to stand, I found that my legs had fallen asleep, and as I rose I collapsed onto the floor. I had to massage my legs for a few moments before I could get myself into a standing position and continue the reading.

꒰ ꒰ ꒰

My character was supposed to take a drink of water. I had a bottle of water with me, so on cue I took a drink from the bottle. It went down the wrong way. I was coughing with water coming out of my nose. The audition had to be stopped because I was choking. I learned then to never drink water at an audition.

꒰ ꒰ ꒰

It was one of my first auditions. I stood before the casting director listening to her directions. She said that I was auditioning for the part of a real bitch. I thought of myself as a nice, quiet person, and suddenly I heard myself saying, "Oh, I couldn't possibly play a bitch! I have no bitchy qualities!" She responded, "Well, in that case you might as well leave right now. Thank you. Next."

I guess I wasn't thinking of myself as an actress yet. What a dope I was!

꒰ ꒰ ꒰

Several years ago I went to a Broadway audition for *Tall Story*, a comedy about a basketball player, the character I was auditioning for. I am six feet tall and thought that wearing lifts in my shoes would add the inches to make me look more like the character. I bought them, put them in, and went to the audition. When I finished my reading the casting director said,

"You're not quite right for this part but you would be perfect for Morty. The only problem is, you're too tall for that character." I shouted out, "No, I'm not that tall, see." I pulled my shoes off and dislodged the lifts, throwing them on the floor, again yelling, "See, see, I'm not that tall." The casting director didn't think what I had done was amusing at all and asked me to leave immediately. As a matter of fact, it appeared that all the auditors looked at me as if I was a crazy person. I felt so humiliated as I picked up my lifts and left. When I got on the street, I dumped them in a trash can.

X X X

I finally decided to buy falsies to enhance what wasn't there. I wore them to an audition. In the middle of the monologue, I squatted and then jumped up, and somehow they dislodged and both popped right out of my square cut blouse onto the floor in front of me. I was mortified, but I continued with the dialogue while retrieving them, and I casually put them back in. I could hear their laughter all the way down the hall to the elevator after I left the room. I never wore them again. And I never auditioned for those auditors again, which was my choice. I couldn't face them.

25.
AFTER-WORDS

I N CONCLUSION, HERE ARE THE THREE BIGGEST CASTING DIREC-
tor complaints, which, presumably, you have uncov-
ered in the reading of this book.

1. Not Being Prepared—the most frequently made mistake
2. Bad Waiting Room Behavior
3. Not Taking Casting Director's Directions

The complaints come from American and Canadian casting
directors. I'm sure British casting directors would concur
with these complaints. You are making the same mistakes no
matter what country you live and train in. Please go back
and read chapters 2, 3, 5, and 7 again.

I must add that I was dismayed by the reluctance of
those casting directors who refused to contribute their input.
Repeated faxes and phone calls made by my assistant to
them were met with either silence or statements such as,
"That's not my bag." I thought, "Is he a man or a fourteen-
year-old boy?" Others declined, replying, "Well, Ginger is a
casting director; she should know. What does she need us to
tell her for?" They totally missed the point. Some said, "I
have my opinions but I'll keep them to myself." They were

obviously not interested in helping actors—and it wasn't *opinions* I wanted; I wanted *facts*. Another response was, "I teach also so why should I tell her?" This book will reach all North American and English actors—her classes are local. "I don't like to be quoted," another one said. If the statement is honest and accurate, then why not, if it benefits actors? "It's none of her business," was another reply.

As can be determined by these responses, not all casting directors are inclined to service actors' best interests—or their own.

Many casting directors wish to be as anonymous as possible to discourage unwanted phone calls, drop-ins, pictures, and résumés. Therefore, they relinquish the opportunity to offer their input or, as in this book, they request that the writer omit their names.

Not to worry. All of the problems we have been talking about can be addressed and, to a greater or lesser degree, solved by you. You can follow the advice in this book, which will broaden your awareness of your own behavior and help you to change the parts of it that may be unacceptable. And you can take some of the steps advised herein to be better prepared for the audition: holding your sides in the most efficient way, dressing to suggest (but only suggest) the character, etc. However, How to Audition classes cannot guarantee you work as an actor, and neither can this book. Acting is an art and a skill, as many of my colleagues and I have reiterated time and time again. If you want to act, you must train.

In the first chapter, and elsewhere in this book, I outline some of the courses that I think are necessary background for a professional actor. There are also dozens of reputable training programs out there, both degree and nondegree. Of course, excellent acting teachers ply their trade in the major actor cities, such as New York, Los Angeles, Chicago, and Toronto, but there are also theatre departments at most of the universities, and some of those will at least provide you with some experience and technique. Not many actors would claim that earning a college degree and adding to their general body of knowledge was a terrible detriment to their careers. David Duchovny has a degree from Princeton; Jodie Foster, Meryl Streep, and Chris Noth have them from Yale; Robin Williams and Christopher Reeve are Juilliard graduates, etc., etc. Recently, especially on television, there has been a real push for younger and younger actors who appeal to the impulse-buying fifteen-to-thirty-nine-year-old demographic so popular with advertisers, and some of those youngsters will no doubt be hired on the basis of hair-teeth-and-bone-structure. Still, if they want to stay in the profession, they will need to learn and grow, just like the rest of us.

To my fellow American actors: there are, in abundance, (in fact, almost all) American (Canadians say "U.S.," never "United States" or "American") films shot on location in Toronto, Vancouver, and throughout Canada. Indeed, I am up here in Toronto teaching Canadian actors how to audition for the American directors who want the same from actors as Canadian directors, only more! American scripts and character breakdowns reflect a more cutting edge to life.

Everyone involved in these productions is American with the exception of the technical crew, day players, and extras, who are Canadian. Casting the leads and featured parts for these films takes place in New York and Los Angeles. Casting for day players and extras takes place in Canada. Canadian actors are not overjoyed about the way these films are cast, and I am sympathetic to their plight. American films financed by American money are under no obligation to hire Canadian actors for leading parts.

Toronto and Vancouver are glorious cities to spend time in and work in. All of Canada is a wondrous country. I hope you get the opportunity to visit and work here.

To my dear Canadian actors: it is unfortunate that there are not more principal and minor principals cast here for

U.S. films. It is assuring for the director to know that he has assembled a first-rate cast of actors whose work he is familiar with before he arrives here. The lesser parts are then filled in with you. However, don't despair. There are those odd times when a minor principal has not been found, and thankfully the director is advised that Canada abounds with highly competent, professional, well-trained, experienced talent. You *do* have a chance to audition for these parts. Those of you with adequate credits on your résumé and with mainstream agents will be granted an audition. The rest is up to you.

For those who get cast in an actor's part, after playing a few of those parts, which will be listed on your résumé, and with a first-rate, mainstream agent to sell you properly and/or if the director remembers you and the Canadian casting director believes in you, there is a very good chance that you will be seriously considered for a principal by the director before he arrives in Canada. All you have to do is give a wonderful audition, and the part is yours!

ABOUT THE AUTHOR

GINGER HOWARD FRIEDMAN is the author of the highly acclaimed *The Perfect Monologue* and *Callback* and has had articles published in New York and Toronto. She has been a Broadway, Off-Broadway, television, and film casting director for several years; has directed on cable television, in regional theatre, and in showcase productions for the industry; is a produced playwright and actress, and has been artistic director of Lone Wolf Productions in New York. She has been teaching her popular "How to Audition/Rehearse" classes in New York, Los Angeles, and Toronto since 1976. Her current and former students include working actors and stars.

Ginger is the founder of the Actors' Audition Training Institute. Currently based in Toronto, she teaches at her studio and throughout Canada. She travels to New York and points south and west to teach at colleges, actors' agencies, and theatre companies. Her videotapes on auditioning are used in universities throughout America. She is a member of the prestigious Toronto Association of Acting Studios, whose members include longtime professional teachers who abide by a written code of ethics.

Ginger has published several essays (not theatre-related), has recently completed a play titled *Just Us and Rita Hayworth*, and is writing a novel.

Ginger is an avid defender of animal rights.